I0831056

Advance Praise for *Life is Lifey*

"Sarah's writing had me laughing out loud from the first line. Funny, addictive, and such a joy to read. At the heart of it all, she's giving women the encouragement to trust their own instincts, which really is the best possible advice out there."

—Krysten Ritter, actress and nationally bestselling author of *Retreat* and *Bonfire*

"*Life is Lifey*'s advice is fresh and handy (no pun intended?) The blowjob tips are 10/10!! Sarah reminds us that being sexy doesn't have an expiration date, and that imperfection? Not only is it totally okay, it's hot."

—Amanda Hirsch, host of critically acclaimed podcast *Not Skinny but Not Fat*

Life is Lifey

THE A TO Z'S OF NAVIGATING LIFE'S MESSY MIDDLE

SARAH SHAHI

A REGALO PRESS BOOK
ISBN: 979-8-89565-028-8
ISBN (eBook): 979-8-89565-029-5

Life Is Lifey:
The A to Z's of Navigating Life's Messy Middle

Cover Design by Conroy Accord

Publishing Team:
Founder and Publisher – Gretchen Young
Editor – Adriana Senior
Managing Editor – Caitlin Burdette
Production Manager – Morgan Simpson
Production Editor – Rachel Paul
Associate Production Manager – Kate Harris

This book, as well as any other Regalo Press publications, may be purchased in bulk quantities at a special discounted rate. Contact orders@regalopress.com for more information.

As part of the mission of Regalo Press, a donation is being made to St. Jude Children's Hospital, as chosen by the author. Find out more about this organization at www.stjude.org.

Regalo Press
New York • Nashville
regalopress.com

Published in the United States of America
3 4 5 6 7 8 9 10

For Wolf, Violet, and Knox. You are the truest loves of my life, the spark in my step, the reason I strive to be better daily. Loving you has stretched me, saved me, softened me, and made me whole. I love you bigger than the sky and wilder than the stars.

For my mother. Mom, your strength is the pulse in these pages. Thank you for raising me with fire and grace. I love you forever.

And to my little Star. You're a daily reminder that great things come in small packages.

Table of Contents

Introduction

What are you going to do? Everything, is my guess. It'll be messy, but embrace the mess. It will be complicated, but rejoice in the complications.... Whatever you choose, however many roads you travel, I hope that you choose not to be a lady. I hope you will find some way to break the rules and make a little trouble out there. And I also hope you will choose to make some of that trouble on behalf of women.

—NORA EPHRON, THE QUEEN OF TURNING HEARTBREAKS INTO BOX-OFFICE GOLD. WATCH HEARTBURN AND YOU'LL BE LIKE, "WOW, PAIN CAN BE HILARIOUS."

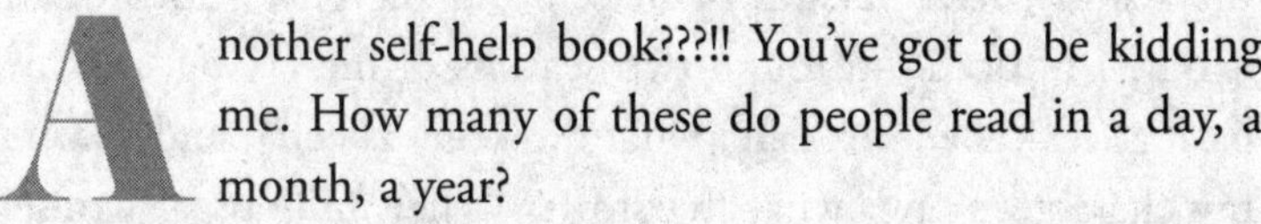

Another self-help book???!! You've got to be kidding me. How many of these do people read in a day, a month, a year?

Well, guess what? I'm not helping you with shit. As a working single mom of three—not my circus, not my monkeys.

OK, I'm kidding, but it's no joke that self-help is a genre that people often roll their eyes at. Here you have someone who acts like they've got everything figured out; they give you IG-worthy pointers on what to do and what not to do in order to #liveyourbestlife.

But life is, well, lifey! It's up and down and all around, and just when you thought you had it figured out—like a punch delivered by the champ himself, POW!—it knocks you sideways. You can have your #bestlife if that's what you want, but I'm more interested in what it means to put the pieces back together in a new shape that fits the person you've become after everything's fallen apart.

Consider me your big sister who's been there before, who wants only the best for you, and who'll love you for exactly who you are, while fearlessly calling you out on your shit.

First, let me introduce myself.

I'm Sarah Shahi. You might know me from my lead role in the globally successful erotic hit on Netflix Sex/Life. Almost overnight, I became the poster child for unhappily married women. Over 170 million people tuned in to watch me take on the role of Billie, who ponders questions about a road not traveled. The viewership continues to grow to this day.

A seemingly happy stay-at-home mom who can't stop reminiscing about the days of old, Billie's haunted by flashbacks of the sparkly, feral version of herself and the guy who brought it out. I noticed—through two seasons of me crying, masturbating (it's called Sex/Life; what did you expect?), and sharing my character's raw "what if?" stories—that millions of women around the world were asking the same questions. They just didn't have the guts or the space to admit it—until now.

As fate so divinely orchestrated, while I was filming Sex/Life, I was going through my own personal transformation. I'd been married for almost twelve years, together for nearly twenty, but my relationship was plagued by problems other than a fantasy man from the past. The years of frustration that came from living a life well below my full potential finally came to a head. I was tired, bloated, and uninspired. The only "self-care" ritual I had was the ten minutes a night I picked food out of my teeth.

In the months leading up to that fateful decision to get a divorce, I wondered to myself, Where did that other girl go? The one who used to chase her ambitions and interests with a sparkly fever was now chasing macaroni noodles from a high chair and adding Metamucil to every meal.

I had settled into a version of myself that made me smaller. But as I came to see, the "other girl" was still there, inside me, waiting to be freed. All I had to do was shut out all the exterior noise and listen. To me.

Who says life can't imitate art? The tides started turning when I filmed the show. Billie became a buzz in my veins. She had the courage to question all the things I had been thinking about. Like me, she was hopelessly flawed and didn't have her shit together. At the same time, she was a devoted mom and a passionate soul with an appetite for a life that was way bigger than the one she was living.

Sex/Life aired in 2021, and within its first three weeks, 69 (a fun and ironic number given the show's content, right?) million people watched. Suddenly, my press became advice columns, and the interviews became therapy. I amassed over 160 million likes on social media from women all over the world who were grateful for a show that made them feel that fucking seen.

So, the unexpected happened: Sex/Life became a battle cry for unsatisfied women who knew in their bones there was something better out there…and I was leading the charge. Women slid into my DMs with questions like: How'd you have the strength to leave? How did you tell your kids? How do you "single-working-mom it"? Many of them would stop me at grocery stores, traffic lights, and my kids' schools, all recounting similar issues. They wanted to turn over a new leaf but didn't have the faintest clue where to start. Many of them felt lost as to how they could find the balls to fully live the life they wanted without giving a fuck what others thought.

Since then, I've been playing therapist to women in multiple languages all across the globe. It's exhausting being me. You try searching for the phrase "Fuck it, you gotta live your life" in Cantonese.

In connecting with women of all ages, races, and backgrounds, something became clear: We're masters when it comes to putting everyone else before us. It's like we took a class on how to disappear into the lives of our husbands and children—so much so that we lose the spark we came into this world with. Because once upon a time, before the diapers, we had dreams. And even if we didn't know exactly how those dreams were going to take shape, we were passionate about living in a way that reflected who we were, deep down: creative, unique, curious, insatiable. That was all before we succumbed to the boring plot of dinner on the table at six.

Lots of the women I've connected with have unhappily assumed the role of multitasking Superwoman (busy at home, busy at work), conveniently eating up the lie most of us were told—that we can "have it all" without some part of our life or inner world suffering as a result. But most of the time, the Superwoman label we've slapped across our foreheads means we're still contorting ourselves into being everything to everyone but not pleasing ourselves in the process. After all, putting our own souls and desires first can be scary because it means digging into the depths with our sharpest machete and a damn good head lamp—and cutting away the debris that's choking out our life energy and killing our spark.

But what's the point of looking like we have our shit together on the outside when we're so tired on the inside that we don't even remember who we are anymore?

Thankfully, as I learned when I left my marriage, every single woman has a superpower at her disposal: her intuition. We don't really need advice from others—a therapist, a friend, an ex, a parent, a neighbor, an Uber driver (fully spilled my guts to one—poor fella). What we do need is permission to wholeheartedly love ourselves: bumps, lumps, and all. We need the time and space to tune in and listen to the wise, bold, smart, awesome woman on the inside whose voice society has taught us to tune out because it's too selfish, too scary, too dangerous, too inconvenient, blah blah blah.

Unsurprisingly, in an era of convenience, we've forgotten how to think for ourselves. We Uber-Eats a Michelin-starred meal to our house, which we just Amazon-Primed a brand-new couch to, all while Netflix tells us what to watch next, and we obey the algorithms that tell us what clothes to buy online. At large, we've lost our ability to think; we've traded in brain cells for swipes and likes.

Life Is Lifey will teach you how to think for yourself again. You'll be offered tips and tricks and personal stories galore that'll help you tune out the peanut gallery and get in touch with your gut. You'll have a front-row seat to your soul and the means to unlock the truth of who you are. All with the help of an occasional kick in the ass to reignite the fire in your belly.

The advice in this book isn't a prescription to help you make decisions more easily or bypass self-doubt. I want you to feel everything—the jagged edges, the glorious a-ha moments, the places where confusion brushes elbows with clarity.

Just be forewarned: Advice is not a one-size-fits-all model. This is gonna read like we're about a tequila deep, sitting on the couch in Xmas PJs (I don't care if it's March, Xmas PJs make everything better—get over yourself), The Great British Bake Off on TV, and a charcuterie board in front of us (if you don't eat cheese, get out). I'll share my stories, my mistakes, and how I found my truest, most connected self amid the misery. I'll help you replace your inner dialogue with your very own unclouded, empowering perspective.

I'm going to share how I weathered my own storms, stayed vulnerable and honest AF about the many ways I screwed up and made right, and hopefully get you not just to nod your head in agreement but to also dig into the inconvenient yet necessary truth of who you are—which means the good, the bad, and the ugly. At the end of each chapter, you'll engage in a soul inquiry through questions that'll help you unlock your own answers. Roll up those sleeves and grab a shovel. We're getting dirty. Obviously, we can't redo the past, but we sure as hell can have a second act that outdoes the first.

Digging into these pages, you'll figure out who the fuck you are, recognize what gives you pleasure, learn your non-negotiables, set boundaries (even when you're scared as shit), speak up for what you want and deserve, and most importantly, trust yourself—especially when you're shaking on the inside and every sentence you utter has a little-girl question mark at the end?

The journey is guaranteed to be messy, and I encourage you to embrace the mess and rejoice in the complications. And grab that tequila! We're gonna be here for a while! Also, you might need a box of Kleenex here and there. But don't worry—I've interjected some funny stories. They're meant to be breathers you can take amidst the heavier moments; growth doesn't have to be so serious all the time! Sometimes we just need to veg out and talk about mind-numbing shit, like where Doja Cat's eyebrows went. Even as we swim the depths of heartbreak, we'll still find time to laugh and dream.

Trust me, even though you probably found this book filed under Self-Help, I'm not here to tell you to suck it up and be more positive. I'm here to help relieve you of the need for perfection. The beauty of life is in the mess. And while we can certainly take responsibility for cleaning up whatever's lurking around on our side of the fence, perfection is never the point—authenticity is.

The second act of your life can be so much richer, so much hotter, so much more exciting than the first because this is the time you're most likely to say, "No more of this shit," and finally consent to living your version of #mybestlife. This is the time you get to break the rules and make a little necessary trouble—not just for yourself, but on behalf of all women. You've already put in all the hard work, and it's time to reap the rewards to become the main character in your script. After all, a miracle is just a shift in perspective—with the help of someone who's got your back every step of the way.

Adulting

"Adulting is an extreme sport. I finally got eight hours of sleep. Took me four days, but whatever."

—PINTEREST

Ugh, "adulting." It's for the fucking birds, I tell you. I used to say the only exciting thing about becoming an adult was finally being able to eat my dessert first. Until five years ago, my life was a snore. It consisted of a daily mundane routine: kids, work, clean, pay the bills, rinse and repeat (notice I didn't say cook, but I'll get to that in a minute), with moments of excitement that were just about as fleeting as the wind.

Is this what I couldn't wait to grow up for? Putting my feelings eloquently, adulting sucked. But in 2020, I was forced to redefine what adulting looked like the moment I closed the door on my eighteen-year union with my ex-husband.

From Mac 'N' Cheese to Life Dreams

I was scared, angry, confused. I had so many questions. *How did I get here? Will I ever meet anyone again?* And the thought that haunted me repeatedly: *Shit, who the fuck is going to cook NOW?*

Visions swirled in my head: my children and me standing alongside the 101 Freeway with a sign reading "not poor, just can't cook," as cars sped by, throwing boxes of Annie's macaroni and cheese at me. My ex was undoubtedly the chef in the family. I never used anything other than a toaster until after the birth of my first child, and even then, my cooking skills ended at boiling water. Once the twins entered the picture, I increased my culinary conquests to microwaveable mac 'n' cheese.

Choosing to walk away from him and the life we shared also meant I chose to walk away from perfectly grilled steaks, mashed potatoes, the juiciest chicken, and a plethora of other mouth-watering meals. Food had been one of our shared love languages, and it was hard to give it up.

But the day had arrived, and I needed to put my big-girl pants on and make something other than the infamous mac 'n' cheese (at least it said "grass-fed cows" on the label). I bought my first set of pans, cooked perfectly burnt steaks, and had three seriously pissed off kids who were convinced I was grilling tires. There were tears (mostly mine), smoke alarms (often), and enough Googling of "why is my steak gray" to qualify for a culinary doctorate in failure. But the persistence finally paid off. One magical Tuesday—I nailed it. The steak was juicy, the potatoes were crispy, and the broccoli wasn't sad. The kids took one bite, paused, and looked at me like I had just performed a miracle. I adulted my way into cooking a real dinner that didn't come out of a box. And then I looked at the sink… Damn.

Hi, my name is Sarah, and I'm an adult now.

Don't Do the Dishes

Let's face it—feeding other humans is hard enough, and trying to juggle *everything else* on top of that? It never ends! Which brings me to this: Being an adult sometimes means making a conscious choice to ignore the chores. Let's start with the dishes.

Whether you are a working mom or the kids are your nine-to-five, chances are you're busier than a fan in July. Maybe tonight, adulting looks like taking something *off* your plate.

Try this on for size: How about *not* doing the dishes? You read that right. This is your permission slip to let them sit! A lot of you may bristle at this idea, but if you can show me where it says that you *must* do the dishes every night after dinner, then I will shit in a bag and punch it.

Instead of rushing all the plates into the kitchen after the last bite is had, use this time to play a board game with the kids, curl up on the couch, and watch shitty TV, or (my personal favorite) climb into bed with a book in one hand and laptop in the other and watch *Hacks* or *Gilmore Girls* with your kids. (BTW, how did Lorelai and Rory find endless amounts of time to get ready in the morning and casually stroll to their heart's content while making it to school and work in time?)

This is *your* night, too, and you get to color it however you want. Trust me, the dishes will still be there in the morning glaring at you as you sip on your cup of joe. Give yourself a break from the domesticity. *That* kind of freedom is also known as adulting.

Being an adult is not *all* about responsibility and chores. Ew, boring. It's about recognizing when you need a break and being adult enough to give it to yourself. It's about realizing when to put the foot on the gas and when to let it off. Some days we wake up, and we just *can't*.

You Write the Rules

According to renowned "adulting" researcher Sarah Shahi, it's about learning how to prioritize these "whatever's necessary" moments. Don't get me wrong—you will still get excited over a new scent of Dawn dish soap, but the beauty of it is this: You get to *choose what each day looks like in order to prioritize a happier YOU.*

It's about sending the kids to bed an hour early when you're desperate to get some quiet time. It's about buckling down and walking headfirst into the shitshow of a day you know you're going to have. Other times, it's about speaking up and giving the other person a big fat piece of your mind. In contrast, adulting can also mean recognizing when *not* to speak up because after all, my dear, you are not the "stupid whisperer."

You can't pour from an empty cup, so of course, adulting includes the mundane parts of life, but it's also about being able to say, "Today we are departing from the regularly scheduled programming because my nervous system needs to *calma* the fuck down!" (All credit goes to Amanda Hirsch for that gem. Look up "Anne Hathaway calma." You're welcome.)

We all know that adulting comes with a long list of pressures—you don't get to sleep in, there's no summer vacation, you have to pay the bills, take care of the children, make the brownies for the bake sale, go to work, feed the dogs, feed the husband, and so on and so forth. That amount of daily pressure is hard!

But when done sanely, we get to *pick* our hard. We're the fuckin' adults, after all.

Turn the Mirror Back on You

Other than having a bottle of Goo Gone under the sink (*adios*, sticky price tags), here are some things to think about that will make adulting a little easier for you.

How did *your* parents "adult"? We mimic how we were raised, so if your parents ran around like the house was on fire, yet the only conflicts on the table were the repairman and your piano instructor arriving at the same time, you may be recreating that level of intensity. Reflect on how you run your day and see where you can afford to go a little slower. You're not your parents, so stop acting like it.

"And on the seventh day, she rested." Just kidding! On the seventh day, she did more cooking, more laundry, and more cleaning than she had Monday through Friday! Time management is an essential part of putting those big-girl pants on. Do not be running just to chase your tail. Be it a day, an afternoon, or even an hour, your time is for you too.

Is there anything you've wanted to learn but haven't? Cooking was always a thorn in my side, and I wasn't going to allow it to poke me any longer. Maybe you want to learn a new language, develop a green thumb, or take a dance class. Turns out, mastering a new skill—or just doing what you love without setting the kitchen on fire—is a totally legit form of adulting.

Aging

"Getting old is like climbing a mountain; you get a little out of breath, but the view is much better."

—INGRID BERGMAN, THE STUNNER FROM CASABLANCA

I was on a show in the mid-2000s (which will remain nameless) working with an actress (let's call her Suzy) whom I had a pretty intertwined storyline with, so we saw each other often. In the mornings, we'd start off in the hair and makeup trailer discussing breaking events, ovulation, and beauty products. She was a good actress and a hard worker, and I appreciated how kind she was to everyone. I had scene partners in the past who were about as cold as a witch's tit, so a day with Suzy was a day well spent.

She was a little older than me and refreshingly open about discussing the work she had done to her face. She was proud of how she looked and was not selfish about sharing how many units of Botox and lip and cheek filler she'd injected. Suzy was like the elder in a tribe but for injections.

One day, I walked into the hair and makeup trailer and saw the entire department surrounding her. Wondering what everyone was gawking at, I walked over to find the ladies marveling at how good her facelift scars were. Damn! This bitch gets it done!

My makeup artist and I walked back to our station as I commented, "I guess this is what you have to do to look good in your fifties."

Her eyes widened, and she whispered back, "Sarah, she's thirty-three!"

Well, strike me pink—you are shitting me, Carol! *Thirty-three*?

The War on Lines

We're told a woman is like a fine wine, and she only gets better with age. Bullshit! Only if you're Elle Macpherson. The societal pressure to look a certain way increases every time you turn on your television or scroll social media. Now more than ever, women have a variety of beauty treatments and surgical procedures at their fingertips that profess to "turn back the clock." Forty is the new twenty; sixty is the new forty. Umm, what happens if you're forty, and you look forty? Is that illegal? Will I be arrested? Charged with aging? *How dare you age?! RUN TO YOUR NEAREST INJECTIONIST, TIFFANY!! THERE'S THIS THING GOING AROUND CALLED WRINKLES. IF YOU CATCH IT, YOU'LL BE LOCKED UP FOR LIFE!*

Yes, life is too short for frown lines, and I love a strategically placed injection. But aging is treated very negatively in our society—like a disease we need to be aware of, so we don't catch it.

The world celebrates the young and rejects the elderly. We will do anything to not become the victims of a sagging chin line and an AARP membership.

But when your entire face morphs into a bloated, smooth, perpetually surprised peach, it makes you look older. I've seen twenty-four-year-olds who I thought looked *great*...for forty-four. So, rock those wrinkles, sister. A line or two never hurt anyone. Sure, a little preservation is fine—but erasing every wrinkle is like wiping out a collection of your best stories. There's no point trying to out-cute the kittens, and it's super cringey when you see an older woman desperately trying to act like she's twenty years younger. Instead, why not be the hottest forty-five, fifty-five, sixty-five-year-old you can be? You're a total badass, and every mark is a medal of honor, not something to delete.

Wrinkles And No Regrets

I was on another job working with a couple of actresses who were both in their twenties. One was twenty-two, and the other was tipping the scales at twenty-seven. Let's call them Daryl 1 and Daryl 2.

First stop of the morning for everyone is always the hair and makeup trailer. A team of experts attacked my face like I was a Formula One race car that had just crashed while they breezed in and out in under fifteen minutes without even wearing under-eye patches. Bitches. They had skin as smooth as glass, lips with the perfect cupid's bow, and full feathery brows that would make a young Brooke Shields jealous.

Daryl 1 and Daryl 2 were always giggling, always sharing inside jokes about last night's wild adventures. I envied a lot more than their skin. While they were up late closing the bar down and hooking up with a set of baby blues, I was pouring MiraLAX in my bedtime drink. They had the kind of energy that I could never get back—the kind of energy that's only found in youth.

Shooting a film is a lot like a marathon, and you have to maintain your stamina, or you'll go as crazy as a hair at the end of a mole. The four-month shoot consisted of fourteen-hour days that were long, slow, and repetitive. As the shoot progressed, the Daryls started unraveling. Their nightly escapades produced drama in their personal lives. Reporting one failed hookup after another, they would come into the trailer crying over some new fuckboy drama. They weren't so easy, breezy, beautiful anymore—and their work suffered because of it. They couldn't remember lines, and their performances were no longer on point, and by the end of the shoot, Daryls 1 and 2, who'd started out as BFFs, couldn't even look at each other.

Now…I love my boring MiraLAX-filled nights! You couldn't pay me enough money to trade places with them. Sure, their skin is tighter, their boobs are more lifted, and there isn't a single dimple in their thighs, but I have something that means so much more than that—the wisdom of experience, which only comes with *age*. Do you know what my wrinkles and my crow's feet mean? Been there, done that, girls. Aging is not just a number; *it's leveling up*.

Self-Love and the Scalpel Are Not the Same

If you're someone who idolizes Jocelyn Wildenstein, a.k.a. the "Cat Lady," then…what's up, pussycat? Meow. But if you're looking to augment your face as a quick fix for self-love, or to please some dumb boy or the unrealistic expectations of society, I will jump in front of that scalpel to tell you: That ain't it, sis. At some point, too much is too much.

Self-love is a messy topic that's thrown in our face more than ever before. Yes, we should love ourselves so much that if we want to change the nose Granny gave us, we should absolutely feel no shame. But how do we experience self-love if we're changing *everything* about us? Is that really self-love? We trade in our mental health for big lips, huge eyes, chiseled cheeks, and feathered brows. Here's an idea—just wear an alien mask. It's about the same thing.

Even our children are starting to experience the pressure on a subconscious level. Skincare is now being targeted towards the youth. It's teaching them to focus on "fixing" themselves before they even know who they are. Can someone explain to me why our nine-year-olds need a serum for "fine lines"? Their only lines are on loose-leaf paper!

What happened to the good old days of slapping on some fruity-smelling lip balm? I mean, my daughter's biggest stress should be whether her best friend likes the same flavor of Gushers—not whether they're a niacinamide or hyaluronic acid girl. Honey, you're neither—you're a KID.

Our preteens don't need retinol; they need self-acceptance. They need to hear that their value isn't tied to how glassy their skin looks or how symmetrical their face is. They need permission to exist exactly as they are.

The glow-up isn't a serum; it's confidence. And confidence doesn't come in a bottle, no matter how cute the packaging is. Their only skincare goal should be washing off glitter and Cheeto dust, not preventing crow's feet before they've even seen a real crow. So, let's toss the mini eye creams, and let kids be kids.

Your Brain Is Your Sex Appeal

I've noticed that any time I feel the most beautiful isn't when my hair, skin, and nails rival Gisele's but when I can hold a conversation that isn't just about my gua sha routine. Sure, everyone wants to look like a cover girl—but how about adding a little cover story to the mix? Because brains? Those don't wrinkle. And being interested in the world around you? That never goes out of style.

You know what doesn't age? A solid opinion on world events, a killer sense of humor, and the ability to make someone laugh until they snort wine out of their nose. You don't get that out of a contour palette.

Read. Get curious about things that light you up and make it a point to learn more about them. Knowing something cool, like how octopuses have three hearts, or being able to recommend the best dumpling spot in town without looking it up on Yelp is the kind of glow people actually stick around for.

So yes, use the serums, dab the concealer, and line the lips—but don't forget to feed your brain while you're at it. Because trust me, there's nothing sexier than someone who can look good and out-argue you about why pineapple doesn't belong on pizza. That's the real timeless beauty secret. Your intellect. That's what really lights up a room.

Turn the Mirror Back on You

Let's get down to brass tacks here. We *all* age. But there's a way to look hot without trying to outrun the clock.

1. Laugh. Laugh hard. Laugh often. Nothing screams *old* like a woman who acts like she's got a stick up her ass.

Stay lighthearted and keep your soul young. Make that left turn instead of the right. For just a second, lose your sense of direction and your mind. Make the kind of memories you can talk about for decades to come. That's where the stories live.

2. No matter what you're injecting into your face, if you're living an unhealthy life, it's gonna show up sooner or later. You want to keep that plumpy Michelangelo cherub skin? Drink more water than wine. Eat for health. Stay away from processed sugar. Get outside and *move*.
3. Want to know the best way to feed your mind? Leave what everyone else is doing behind and pursue *your* interests. Love yoga? Get certified. Want to learn something new but don't know where to start? The internet is your friend! You can basically find an affordable online class on any topic imaginable. Online learning portals like Udemy can give you the lowdown on whatever you want—from learning how to plant seasonal flowers in your own Zen garden, to figuring out WTF your dog or cat is trying to communicate to you, to understanding why *Mean Girls* still explains 90 percent of female friendships. Life is happening all around you. Take an interest. You have a lot more to give than what people see on the outside.

Blowjobs

"Learn to love the blowy, and your guy will be obsessed with you."

—ME

"LADIES—LISTEN HERE—the sloppier, the wetter, the better. Moan and groan, and choke on that dick!"

No, this was not some bizarre, meant-to-be-motivational-but-kinda-just-weird workout chant. Those words were commanded by Lou Paget, the author of the infamous *The Big O*, as I sat in her blowjob class in 2000. I had just moved to LA from Texas, met a cute boy, and my inexperienced self quickly got the hint that he wanted more than just dry humping. Let's call him Boyfriend: ten years older, desirable, and a critically acclaimed (in his mind) B+ movie star. I was determined to make him a *happy* boyfriend. Thus, my virginal, chaste, Southern, sheltered, Persian upbringing days needed to come to an end.

"These dicks aren't gonna ejaculate themselves; let's get started!"

I appreciated this strangely upbeat sentiment for the situation as a respectable six-inch dildo was served in front of me on fine china. At twenty, easily the youngest in attendance, I was surrounded by a group of women in their thirties and forties who needed help unleashing their inner Christy Canyon. Through instructional hand and mouth techniques, Lou broke down the penis in a way that made my analytical, overthinking, inexperienced mind feel safe to be my very own porn star.

The class was a two-day seminar, turning us all into certified pros in the fine art of hand and mouth techniques. We covered everything from the anatomy of a penis (nerve endings galore) to pacing, deep-throating, lubrication, and exactly how much pressure to apply. By the end, I was so damn confident I felt like I could deep-throat a cactus. But it wasn't just about mastering the technique—it was about giving the whole situation the kind of attention that turns a regular day into a national holiday.

Spoiler alert: Mr. Boyfriend was absolutely thrilled.

But It Looks Like an Angry Pirate

It wasn't always like that. I used to be intimidated by the one-eyed willy. I was raised in the South by a Persian single mom and had the fear of God put into me about the danger of engaging in premarital affairs. "You will go straight to hell, and your vagina will fall off! Now, back to your times table!"

Aside from my kindergarten romance where we exchanged juice boxes like wedding vows, I got my first boyfriend when I was fourteen. Let's call him First Boyfriend. He was lovely and sweet and on the receiving end of a lot of over-the-pants handies. I certainly wasn't ready to even make eye contact with his willy let alone put my hands on it, so I thought it was a great compromise. Any time he was over, I always kept the door open just to ensure he wouldn't try anything I wasn't ready for (now that I think about it, I may even remove my children's room doors altogether until they're forty), and if he couldn't whip it out, his membrane down under didn't exist! GENIUS! Alas, like most high school flings, ours couldn't make it past the cafeteria doors.

A few years later while I was a freshman at Southern Methodist University, I met another amour. He was older, had facial hair, and his father definitely didn't have to drive us to our dates. A step up from First Boyfriend. One night, after a dazzling date at The Mansion on Turtle Creek, he wanted to come back to my dorm room. My roommate was always there, so I figured I'd escape the chances of anything sexual happening.

We get to my room…and hold on a sec…what the fuck?! The bitch isn't there!!?? And the door doesn't stay open! It was one of those heavy doors that automatically closed! Shit. Fuck me sideways! Actually, no—don't! At all! We walk in, the door slams shut, and my heart drops out of my body. We start kissing, and that motherfucker was so sly, I didn't even hear him unzip his pants as he brought his peen out. There it was, full of veins and rumpled skin, standing at attention, glaring back at me with its one piercing eye. And why are parts of it dark? EW! I'm supposed to *want* to touch that? NOPE.

This being the first time I had ever seen one, my initial instinct was to scream—full-on Janet Leigh in *Psycho*—and run down the hall wailing, "Stranger danger!" Instead, I tried to appear cool, calm, and like I saw dicks morning, noon, and night. My rationale from my days with First Boyfriend kicked in: *If I don't make eye contact, it's not there! Brilliant!* All while a flurry of thoughts went through my mind: What do I do? Do I pet it? Do I blow on it? Does it respond to a whistle?

After a few awkward minutes, the owner of this membrane averted eye contact with me, kissed me on the forehead, and off he went. Never heard from him again. Wonder why.

Learn to love the blowjobs, sister. And it's not just for the receiver; it's empowering to take your partner to ecstasy. *You* are in control of *their* pleasure, so pleasing them should be fun for you, too. Whether you learn through a class, conversations with your girlfriends, or a book, the thing that you may be dreading could turn out to be your helping hand (pun intended). Sure, they're called "jobs" for a reason (cue Samantha from *Sex and the City* almost three decades later), but on those nights that you couldn't be bothered—where you were the first one up with the kids and the last one to put them to bed, where even the hands of Tom Brady himself would get slapped away—learning how to properly deep-throat that sucker will be good for him *and* you. But you *must* commit! Spit on it, make it sloppy, gag (every guy wants to think his "down under" is just too big for his wittle lady's mouth), and make subtle little groans that even Stormy Daniels would applaud. You'll have a very happy partner in under ninety seconds, and you, my dear, will still have enough time to cuddle up in bed reading your book by nine.

Turn the Mirror Back on You

Sister, I get it. There are other things you'd rather do than give head. But ask yourself *why* you don't like giving your man a blowy. If we can break down the barriers and reframe it in a way that the BJ is your literal helping hand, you will not only make him happy, but you'll be even happier. Handjobs are acceptable too, but I'm all about efficiency. It's the lazy girl's way of having sex.

So, now to the barriers:

1. Hygiene issues are the number-one reason most women don't open up and say "ahhh." If so, tell your beau to take a shower—but don't say it in an offensive way. "Your shit constantly stinks. Take a shower; I'll blow you." Try using your best whispery, phone sex operator voice: "Hey baby, do you want to pop in the shower? I've got a surprise for you when you come out." He won't mind if he knows what's coming after.
2. Is your guy's peen a scary-looking membrane with a sharp curve to the right and just a bitch to look at? Well, close your eyes! HA! No, seriously, if you can look at it from a biological standpoint, the penis has different sections, all of which are very sensitive. Breaking it up anatomically keeps you honed in on each section individually, and you won't have to see it as one overwhelming shebang.
3. Are you afraid of deep-throating? Yes, I know, it's very counterintuitive to open up to the thing that makes you gag. But this is the key to a mind-blowing blowy: You have to somewhat desensitize your gag reflex and open up your throat. Either with a toothbrush or your finger (obviously nothing big that would get stuck), touch the back of your throat and see if you can hold the object there for maybe five seconds. When giving a blowjob and activating the gag reflex, you produce a lot of saliva. Use that to your advantage. The wetter the better. A dry tug is no fun.

Boundaries Bitch

"Lack of boundaries invites lack of respect."

—SOMEONE SO OLD WE CALL HIM/
HER "ANONYMOUS"

Kids are hungry—have to feed them (so annoying). Hubby had a rough day—needs consolation (takes more damn work than the kids). Friend's husband just left her—time for a three-hour group chat where everyone voodoo-dolls the shit out of him (no, of course you don't hate him; you just hope he gets hate-fucked by a shark).

And then…

You put the kids to bed, sit on the couch, and pour a glass of wine when…damn it…you remember your neighbor's out of town, and you volunteered to take care of their cat (*whyyyyyy* did you do that?). You rush over in your cat pajamas and slippers to make sure the pussy is fed. Finally, you crawl into bed, close your eyes—fuuuuuuck! You're head of the talent-show committee, and you forgot to send the emails about rehearsal tomorrow...so now, you gotta drag your ass to your computer and take care of business.

Alright, REM, here you come...almost there...until a teeny voice on the other side of the door wakes you up.

"Mommyyyyyyyy..."

Groan. Punch pillow. It's gonna be a long night.

Wine or the hard stuff? It's five o'clock somewhere, right?

Polite's Not Always Right

Before we became the savage, magical badasses we are today, we were coached to be people-pleasing machines: Put others first, smile when we want to throw a shit fit, and never, ever talk back. Hate to break it to you but not exactly a crash course in empowerment.

I used to think saying no to someone's request for my time meant I was a little cunt-flap. My over-giving Persian upbringing was only magnified by growing up in Texas, where they wear their Southern hospitality with pride. If a truck ran me over, I'd apologize for being in its way. If my phone started nagging at me, I'd drop whatever I was doing to answer a call or return a text. Otherwise, I'd be the worst person in the world for failing to return their message a nanosecond later. As my upbringing taught me, put others first, right?

However, something shifted over the years, most likely due to the fact that I had more bags under my eyes than in my closet. Though that double X chromosome means I am superhuman, I am not a superhero. I'm not able to fly around town living everyone else's best life *and* my own. I can't go from friend to child to partner to pet making service calls: "Yes, we can do the playdate after school. Sure, we can get sushi for dinner. I'd love to clean the kitchen. Oh, it would be my pleasure to give you a blowjob when the kids go down! And of course, I have time to meet up for a quick drink to bash your crazy ex-husband!"

There's no way we can possibly please everyone—and if we're trying, we're the ones who'll inevitably be fucked. Break up with that childhood conditioning to always be "nice." Your main character era doesn't have room for that now.

Born a Doormat

In January 1988, my mother was in labor with my personal sandwich-maker, a.k.a. my sister Samantha. Daddy dearest dropped Mom off at the Hurst-Euless-Bedford Hospital—and instead of following her into the delivery room to gaze into the beautiful deep-brown eyes of his newborn baby girl, he took off the moment she was wheeled in and sped off to his drug dealer in Mexico (insert gasping sound here... *GASP*).

A year of me sitting by the window patiently waiting for his black Caddy to pull into the drive went by before I saw him again (insert horrified chorus of "oh-no-he-didn't" here). His appearances were weird—like a hemorrhoid—awkward, uncomfortable, and always showing up at the worst possible time. Thankfully, they were also rare. Still, every time he showed, I wrapped myself around him and catered to his whims—anything to keep him from leaving. I believed that if I tried hard enough, I could hold him in place. But of course, I couldn't.

At eight years old, I hadn't yet realized that no amount of love could make me a superhero. I had no control over the comings and goings of a volatile, addicted adult who happened to be my father. I was just a kid. Hopelessly human.

But it was too late. Then and there, a doormat was born.

Cue my abandonment issues! They were now center stage, running the show. For a large portion of the thirty-two years that followed, I perfected my people-pleasing tendencies by putting everyone else first just so they wouldn't abandon me.

"Mom, can I clean the whole house and iron your sheets before starting my homework? And would you be proud if I signed up for swim team? I may drown from exhaustion, but at least you won't leave me, right?"

"Dad! Good to see you again. How was Mexico? Get any good drugs? Yes, I'll tell Mom to file for divorce if that'll make you happy. That's exactly the kind of stuff we nine-year-olds talk about with our moms, anyway!"

My people-pleasing trickled down to my friends, too. When they wanted to play Barbie, guess who got stuck being Ken? Yep, me. Sure, I'll be the smooth, anatomically incorrect male doll with zero wardrobe options. That's every little girl's dream, right? Forget the Dreamhouse—I'll just stand off to the side while Barbie drives the convertible.

I'd shut down my own feelings just to feel "chosen." God forbid I spoke up and said, "Hey, I'm tired of being Ken. Can I be Barbie this time?" The fear was real—what if they called me "selfish" and kicked me out of the Barbie Dream Squad? Back then, being called "selfish" felt like the ultimate death sentence. For lil' goody-two-shoes Sarah, that word was basically a one-way ticket to social exile. Call Jesus—I'm coming home!

So, as the overachieving, highly ambitious, career-gal people-pleaser I morphed into, I somehow decided that being a "good person" meant doing *literally everything.* Since the age of eight, my life became a never-ending triathlon of juggling other people's needs, fixing their problems, and making sure their emotional support cups were overflowing—meanwhile, mine was bone-dry.

And then a few years ago, one dismal, emotionally exhausting, tear-filled day (back then, crying was nothing out of the ordinary—it could've been a Tuesday, and if the grapes were staring at me sideways, waterworks), I was listening to Oprah's *Super Soul Sunday*, and I heard her break down the word "selfish" into something that didn't mean I was a shitlord for wanting to prioritize my own needs. Oprah described selfishness as a state of being "full of one's self." And if *you* weren't full of *you*, who else would be?

Jaw. Drop.

Wait, the high priestess herself is saying it's *good* to be selfish? How the fuck did I go my whole life without getting *that* memo? According to Oprah, there was nothing more beautiful than being selfish because it meant you were actually inhabiting your *full* self.

Most of us were born with blurry lines and big hearts, and we need to be reminded to take care of ourselves—because we're important, too! You're not here to wait on everyone hand and foot, and you're not a bad person for setting boundaries for yourself! And if you're labeled a "bitch," great! You'll just be a more energized one!

Think Twice About Being Nice

Whether it's with our kids, our spouse, or strangers on the street, we teach people how to treat us. It's a hard pill to swallow, but it's actually very simple: *We get what we allow.* So, if you want to receive something different than what you're getting, don't allow it.

My life got better when I realized I don't have to be nice. Constantly acting like the sun was shining out of my ass just to make others happy took its toll. Nice got me run over time and time again.

Now, the person I'm nice to the most? Me.

Boundaries are self-care. You can say no with respect and gentleness, and there's no need to explain yourself. Because, as Anne Lamott- my literary crush and queen of no-bullshit spiritual wisdom- said, "'No' is a complete sentence." It's essential to protect your mental health, so you can show up like a cup of fucking sunshine for those who need you most. Otherwise, you're cloudy with a chance of rain…indefinitely.

Verbal Boundaries with Morons

It's not only your time that can be taken advantage of. Sometimes, a rude comment will slice you up if you're not careful. Setting verbal boundaries with those who are disrespecting you is crucial.

Let's just say your inappropriate Uncle James makes a comment about your ass looking bigger than a double-wide at Christmas. Here's an appropriate response to shoot back with: "Uncle James, that's an odd thing to say out loud. I don't tell you those pants make your dick look small."

OK, maybe you're not there yet, and that's cool. Baby steps. Here's a less biting version: "Uncle James, that's an odd thing to say out loud. Does putting someone else down make you feel better?" Attack the insult directly, point out how inappropriate it is for them to be voicing it, and question their judgment.

Maybe your boss is questioning your IVF journey, and it's not something you prefer to discuss around the water cooler.

"That's a really personal question, Mr. Titler, and I'd rather not discuss it." Walk away feeling fantastic knowing you set a verbal boundary for yourself. Mr. Titler does *not* get to ask you about your pregnancy journey if you don't want him to.

Nicole, the class mom who tries to one-up everyone with her famous brownies and always-open schedule, offers a double-edged compliment about your new haircut at pickup: "You look really nice! That new 'do makes your nose look smaller." Give 'em your best Clint Eastwood stare and say, "What do you mean by that?" Address the part of the comment that was meant to belittle and watch her squirm. Then, when her kid comes out, you can say, "I'm sure you meant that in the nicest way possible. Hopefully, you'll teach your daughter to do better," and walk away with your head held high, big nose and all. Ha ha! Nicole didn't get you this time!

Turn the Mirror Back on You

It's better to recognize when you need a break than to have a breakdown. So, ask yourself the following:

1. Are you tired of feeling like you're doing things for everyone but never getting anything done for yourself? Look at everything on your to-do list and see where you can make some cuts. You're allowed to say, "I'd love to do this, but maybe another time." The people who love you will never make you choose between self-care and them.
2. Are you overly concerned about people liking you? It probably started when you were a kid, trying to win gold stars from a teacher or family member. But guess what? You definitely don't need anyone's approval to

live your life. Trust me, the opinions of others aren't the VIP pass you think they are.

3. Remember, "No" is a complete sentence. It is perfect in and of itself. When you say it, you essentially convey, "I've given enough." No ifs, ands, or buts necessary.

Comparison

"Today you are you, that is truer than true. There is no one alive who is you-er than you."

—DR. SEUSS. FUN FACT, HE WASN'T FOND OF KIDS.

Did your parents ever compare you to your brown-nosing sibling? Did Miss Goody Two Shoes make straight As, and all you heard was, "Why can't you be more like your sister?" as if having a high GPA was a personality trait? Or maybe it wasn't your family—it was your best friend. She always got the guy *you* liked. Why? Because she had shiny, shampoo-commercial hair, and her parents dropped her off in a sleek black Jeep. Meanwhile, you rolled up in a squeaky minivan with a bumper sticker that said, "My kid is an honor roll student," and braces that made you look like you swallowed a slinky. Let me let you in on something you may not have thought about: Comparing yourself to others puts the focus on the wrong person. It's an absolute waste of time. Like taking a shit, and then trying to shove it back up there. But why?

The urge to compare was injected into your subconscious mind at an early age. Comparisons sneak up and drag us down long after the moment's passed. We woulda-coulda-shoulda ourselves into a full spiral, and before you know it, you're questioning every choice since sixth grade. Why? Because we all have a primal need to feel accepted. We want to be loved as we are—but sometimes, we get so busy trying to fit in, we forget who we *truly* are.

Here's the thing: When that stork dropped you off on Mommy and Daddy's doorstep, maybe you were a little bit shy of winning the genetic lottery, but you were *still* as shiny as a new penny. It's time to stop comparing yourself to others and start remembering that *being authentic beats being perfect every single time.*

Everyone is blessed with a set of gifts and a way of viewing the world that's uniquely their own. Maybe you have a photographic memory, don't experience period pain, or can actually lick your elbows. Whatever it is, you were put on this planet to live out the fullest expression of you. Deciding that someone else's gifts are better than yours is the quickest way to rob yourself of joy. Who cares if someone is prettier, skinnier, smarter, or they have bigger boobs, a smaller nose, more money, a better job—are you happy with *you*? It is a waste of your precious time to spend one single moment measuring yourself against anyone else! Why deny the world your individuality by trying to conform? We need *you.* Just the way you are.

"WAP" by Celine Dion

Okay, it doesn't exist, but it's a smashing subtitle, am I right? But let's entertain this for a second. What if Cardi B compared herself to Celine Dion? Can you even imagine what "WAP" would've sounded like? Picture Cardi on a wind-blown cliff, eyes closed, channeling full *Titanic* drama while rapping about…well, things that would've made Jack and Rose blush. Go ahead, I'll wait.

Exactly! It doesn't work. Because trying to fit into someone else's melody will always throw you off *your* rhythm. You've got to chase yourself down like a squirrel on a mission for its last stash of nuts—relentless, wild, and fully you. Have the *cojones* to show up in your truest form, instead of molding yourself into what you *think* others will like. Stop editing your essence. You don't need to shape-shift for approval. The right people will recognize the unfiltered version—you just have to be brave enough to bring it.

Sister, comparing our weaknesses to someone else's strengths is a recipe for disaster. Don't deny the world the magic you carry. Whether you're Team Cardi or Team Celine, you do you. Stay in touch with your weird. You're the absolute tits just the way you are, so act like it already!

I Can Buy Myself Flowers

When I was a teen, I did show choir. I was like Rachel Berry in *Glee* but less cunty. Humble-not-so-humble brag here: I always had the solos, and I was always the star. After every performance, parents would swarm their children with flowers, balloons, and endless praise. I would find my mother, with my baby sister in tow, standing at the back of the auditorium empty-handed.

"Why didn't you bring *me* any flowers? Carey's parents bought *her* a bouquet!" I hounded her with the same question for five years, seventh through twelfth grade.

She always answered with the same response. "Did you think you were good?"

"Fuck yeah, I was, bitch! Did you see how my eyes dazzled up there? The audience was mesmerized! What's wrong with you?" OK, fine, I didn't say those *exact* words. It was something more like, "Yeah." And she'd reply with, "Then you don't need flowers. You have your own approval, and that's enough." Ugh, no mom, *flowers* would have been enough. My own approval doesn't smell as nice as *roses.*

It wasn't until later in life, when I was on everyone's favorite lesbian soap opera, *The L Word*, that I understood the power of that lesson. During one of the scenes, a guest actress on the show had to cry. Over and over again, she would ask the director for approval, and between takes, she would ask *me,* "How did you feel that came across? Did you see the water in my eyes? Could you feel my pain?" (Roll your eyes, please; actresses can be so fucking ridiculous.) *She didn't have her own approval, so she hunted for it from everyone else.*

I answered with how amazing she was in the same way you compliment a toddler's crayon drawing: "Wow. That was amazing. Did you do that all by yourself?" It was exhausting. As Travis Tritt so eloquently sang, "Here's a quarter—call someone who cares."

Later in the season, my character Carmen was left at the altar by everyone's favorite fuckgirl—her beloved Shane. Now, it was my time to turn on the waterworks. Between takes, I stayed focused and quiet, listened to a bunch of sad songs, and thought about puppies dying—and I *nailed* it. I never asked how I did or if the camera caught how wet my bottom lashes were. The only thing that was real to me in those moments was that the love of my life was abandoning me on my wedding day.

It was in that moment that I learned the lesson my mother had been trying to teach me years earlier. If *I* thought I crushed it, I didn't need to ask for approval or measure my success against anyone else's. I was happy with my work and that was mine to hold. Validation is cute and all, but you know what's cuter? Knowing you're a boss without needing the world to clap for it. I am my own judge and jury. I don't need to chase an applause, because I give myself a standing ovation. I can buy my own damn flowers.

Wake Up, Bitches! Stop Scrolling

The rabbit hole of social media is a dangerous spiral with no shovel at the bottom to dig yourself out. Listen up, peanut, stop scrolling! The amount of time we spend allowing bat-shit crazy thoughts to multiply wildly in our brain is a colossal waste of our time. How do I know? Because I've been there. I used to scroll, like, and check those DMs before my alarm could even *finish* ringing.

It's hard not to get jealous of everyone with a curated newsfeed who's waking up on a yacht in Italy while you're looking at your fancy view of the 405 Freeway, and Leonardo DiCaprio sure as fuck isn't rubbing sunscreen into the small of your back. But hey, if you want to live a life you've never lived, you've got to do things you've never done.

Look, just try it! Cut back on social media. Studies show that the less time you spend scrolling, the happier, lighter, and more productive you'll feel. I'm not saying you have to quit cold turkey, but set some limits. If you're a morning scroller, like I used to be, here's an idea: When your alarm goes off, *don't* reach for Instagram. Instead, hit yourself with an affirmation like, "I'm a badass bitch, and today is going to go exactly how I want it to," or, "Why am I so amazing? Why are my tits so perky?" Trust me, starting your morning off by hyping yourself up is **chef's kiss*.

I'd much rather boost my own vibe at the start of the day than compare my 3D life to some celeb's filtered post about sipping their espresso in their villa in Mallorca, while pretending they just "woke up like this"—when we all know it took two hours, one lighting assistant, and at least three passive-aggressive arguments to nail that casual morning aesthetic. And let's be real: That croissant from their "candid" shot isn't even warm anymore, and I'm pretty sure that villa smells like cheap tanning lotion and regret.

The moment you start comparing yourself to someone else's curated fairytale, you forget that your *real* life can be as amazing as you decide to make it.

And *your* croissant...is warm.

Turn the Mirror Back on You

The desire to be someone else is a waste of the person you are. Reclaim your badassery, sis.

1. Put your phone down and stop doom-scrolling your ex's new girlfriend. Protect your peace. Instead, go find a mirror and look yourself in the eye—*that's* the woman who deserves your attention. You get 86,400 seconds every single day. Don't waste a single one of them believing you're anything less than amazing.

2. Focus on your strengths. Write down the things you're amazing at: Maybe you're a pro at reading people, a top-tier cook, or you make playlists so good they could change lives. Me? I cry. All. The. Time. For years, I thought it made me weak. But plot twist: My emotions are my superpower. Know how I know? I'm the friend everyone calls when their life is falling apart. Emotional intelligence for the win, baby. So, figure out what makes you *you* and make it work for you. Your weird little quirks? That's where the magic is.
3. When you start comparing yourself to others, remind yourself of all the badass things you've done—big and small. Sure, you might not have a private jet, but your kid told you your mashed potatoes were "literally perfect," so you're a Michelin-star chef in their eyes. Remember that roller-skating party you threw for your ten-year-old? The one he's still talking about? Yeah, you're a party-planning legend. You're not just making a mark; you're creating core memories over here. Those last longer than anything money can buy.
4. Want an easy hack to stop comparing? Fan another sister's flame! Toot other people's horns in addition to your own. Tell that woman on the sidewalk she's killing it. Buy a latte for your coworker who just nailed the presentation she was stressed over. Not only does it feel good to pay a compliment forward, but it's all just awesome energy that comes back to you in the end! Compliments are the ultimate currency—spend generously!

Courage

"Life shrinks or expands in proportion to one's courage."

—ANAÏS NIN, A LITERARY BOSS. SHE JUGGLED TWO HUSBANDS—AT THE SAME TIME—AND NEITHER OF THEM KNEW. SHE ALSO WAS ONE OF THE FIRST IN WESTERN LITERATURE TO SHOCK THE WORLD WITH EROTIC FICTION.

"I finally love myself more."

Those five words took ten years to say. My voice shook the whole time. "I do love you," I repeated, "but I finally love myself more."

With tears cascading down my face, I'd just told my husband of eleven years that I wanted a divorce. I wanted to leave the life we'd shared for more than eighteen years with three healthy children and a cute little rescue dog to do life on my own. I hadn't been on my own since I was twenty-two. I was now forty. And my tits weren't as perky. Now *that's* courage.

Let's get Webstery for a second. Courage is defined as the "strength of mind to carry on in spite of danger or difficulty." It's the balance between our inner and outer selves. As Maya Angelou—the literary powerhouse whose words have shaped my heart more than anyone's—once said, "Courage is the most important of all the virtues because, without courage, you can't practice any other virtue consistently. You can practice any virtue erratically, but nothing consistently without courage."

Without courage, you wouldn't dare fall in love, go after that dream job, pack your bags for the city that's been calling your name, or finally launch that business idea you can't stop thinking about. You wouldn't demand your worth, take the unbeaten path, or open the door to new possibilities. Courage is the mother of all progress, but here's the kicker: Your brain *hates* change. *We are wired to choose a familiar hell over an unfamiliar heaven,* so we have to actively make a decision to do the shit that feels daunting and uncomfortable. Courage is something we have to *practice.* READ THAT LAST SENTENCE AGAIN. It's a muscle you have to flex. We have to *actively choose* to do the shit that scares us—because just on the other side of fear is everything you've ever wanted.

After several award-worthy performances of being a scaredy cat myself, I learned that courage isn't the absence of fear; it's feeling the fear and walking right into it anyway. You have to be brave enough to listen to that little voice within that's urging you to be more than what you are. No matter what any Julia Roberts movie from the '90s might say, happily ever after is a work in progress, and the life you want isn't gonna fall out of the sky and plop into your lap with the wave of a fairy godmother's wand. You'll need to venture out of your cocoon and into the dark, swampy forest if you want to find the treasure.

Don't Do the Same Thing Over and Over and Call It a Life

In 2017, the TV show I was starring in got canceled. The ratings? Let's just say we had about as many viewers as Yoko Ono would on opening night at Madison Square Garden. Oh, what's that? You didn't know she sang? Exactly.

Up until then, I'd had a solid thirteen-year run in network television. I was a reliable "network darling," but deep down, I was *miserable.* I didn't leave my entire family behind in Texas, quit Southern Methodist University *and* the Dallas Cowboys Cheerleaders just to spend a decade furrowing my brow and saying, "The suspect is in custody," on various network crime shows. That wasn't the dream. I was only using a fraction of my potential, and by "fraction," I mean I was the space between commercials on network tv.

I wanted more. I wanted cable. I wanted accents. I wanted period pieces. I wanted to say "fuck" like it was punctuation. It was time for a career makeover.

But here's the snag in my Spanx: Being the reliable network sweetheart I was, none of the fancy, edgy cable shows would touch me. In Hollywood terms, I wasn't a *real* actress—I was the filler between Colgate and Geico. And let's be honest, that's not sexy.

So, I had to flip the script on how Hollywood saw me. And let me tell you, this was no easy task. For an entire year, I did the unthinkable: I said *no* to every single network job that came my way. Yep. Every. Single. One. Buttercup, that took superhero-sized balls of steel.

And trust me, it wasn't pretty. Watching those roles go to younger, hotter actresses? BRUTAL. My agents? Fully panicked. They practically staged an intervention. "Think of the exposure! Think of the *opportunities*!" they cried. The network execs were equally confused. "Wait, Sarah turned that down? Is she OK? Does she…need meds?"

Was I scared? Fuck yes, I was! Fear was in my ear twenty-four seven whispering, "What if you're making a huge mistake? What if you never work again? Maybe you *do* need meds." My career felt like it was teetering on the edge of a cliff, and I was the one holding the scissors to the safety net.

But every time I considered saying "yes" to another safe, shiny network gig, I felt I'd be diving headfirst back into the very pit I was clawing my way out of. My agents urged me to "think of the opportunities," but all I could feel was the weight of the compromise. It wasn't a step forward; it was a slow slide back into a version of myself I was trying to outgrow.

Fear is a sneaky little gremlin—it wears logic like a disguise and whispers things like "Don't be stupid. Take the role, idiot. What if you never work again?" But I knew better. Playing it safe had gotten me stuck. I had to tap into something more defiant, more *me*. So I channeled my inner outlaw—the part of me that didn't shrink, didn't people-please, and definitely didn't settle. Trailblazers don't back down just because the road ahead looks empty.

So yeah, I took my place at the very back of the unemployment line, metaphorically singing for my supper. But this time, I wasn't serenading any old network exec—I was belting it out for HBO, Netflix, Showtime…you get the vibe.

And for almost a year? Crickets. Nada. In Hollywood, silence isn't just awkward—it's lethal. Off the radar is basically a death certificate for your career, unless you're planning a scandal, a facelift, a strategic "accidental" paparazzi moment, or launching a wellness brand. My agents? Spiraling. "Should we get her a lobotomy? Botox? A TikTok dance lesson?"

And then—just when I was about to lose all hope or launch a line of crystal-infused protein bars—the universe finally threw me a bone: an audition for a gritty Showtime series set in the '90s, produced by Matt Damon and Ben Affleck, starring Kevin Bacon, called *City on a Hill*. It had all the things I'd been craving: edge, depth, and lots of "fucks."

After a year in career purgatory, I walked into that room with a chip on my shoulder the size of Los Angeles. Funny enough, that's *exactly* who the character was—cold, snarky, and royally pissed at the world.

I booked it.

Suddenly, I was swearing in every episode, rocking acrylics like a Real Housewife, and diving headfirst into messy, scandal-filled storylines. And bonus, it was on cable! When the show aired, critics around the world were like, "Wait a second… Sarah Shahi, "the network actress," can pull off a period piece? *And* a Boston accent? Who knew?" (Me. I knew.)

But just as I was getting into my cable TV groove, life hit me with another plot twist: My character was only contracted for one season. FUCK! So, after *City on a Hill* ended, I found myself back in what felt like the never-ending chokehold of Hollywood. My options? Jump into yet another network crime drama where I could utter riveting lines like "We've got a lead on the suspect," or stay jobless and spiral into the abyss. Guess which one I chose? Yep, the abyss. I started asking myself the hard questions: "Am I ever going to get the edgy, character-driven work I dream about or is this it? How much is a facelift?"

Then, fast-forward to January 2020, and the universe finally coughed up the goods. I booked *Sex/Life* on Netflix. The show premiered, and suddenly, 170 million people were watching me live out the beautifully chaotic woes of Billie Mann. I got to cry, curse, make questionable life choices, and say a lot more than "fuck." And just like that, my years of saying no to what didn't align *finally* paid off.

The moral of the story, sis? It takes *guts* to stand up for what you believe in. You have to be willing to fail, to be rejected, to sit through endless awkward silences and career dry spells. But in the words of Samuel Beckett: "Try again. Fail again. Fail better."

You don't gain anything by risking nothing. So, fall. Fall in love, fall in pain. Fall in loss, fall in gain. No matter where you land, at least you had the fortitude to get moving. Don't busy yourself doing the same old thing you've always done. Robin Sharma said it best: "Don't live the same year seventy-five times and call it a life."

On another note, this courage mixed with a dash of outlaw was exactly what led me to become a Dallas Cowboys Cheerleader....

Jump and the Net Will Appear

I was doing my best Rachel Berry (yes, from *Glee*, keep up!) while attending Southern Methodist University in Dallas. I was in a musical production of *Soapdish*, and everyone in the cast knew two things about me: I wanted to be an actress, and I had absolutely no clue how to make it happen. Honestly, figuring out how to roller-skate on the moon seemed easier than landing a yogurt commercial.

One of the dancers in our cast casually suggested I try out for the Dallas Cowboys Cheerleaders. Why? Because in 1995, they'd been on *Saturday Night Live*. That was my logic: *Saturday*

Night Live is acting; cheerleading gets you on *Saturday Night Live*. Boom. My way in!

Now, let me be clear: I knew nothing about cheerleading. But as an Aries rising, I am legally obligated to say yes to wildly ambitious ideas, so I thought, *What's the worst that could happen? I don't make it? Big deal, I'll survive.*

HOLY SHIT. Cut to 472 hopefuls including me standing outside Texas Stadium on a blistering summer day, all vying for the coveted title of "often imitated, never duplicated" Dallas Cowboys Cheerleader. Most of them were professional dancers who had been pirouetting since they were in diapers. Me? My last dance class was Hip Hop for Beginners. When I was five.

But I had to be stronger than my mind. *SNL* was just on the other side of my fear!The audition process was months long with multiple cuts after each round. My fear of being the double left-footer forced me to work harder than everyone else, so I was always among the first ones there and the last ones to leave. We would line up, single file, while the choreographers yelled out turns and moves, and one by one, we went across the floor displaying them. I stood at the back of the line, where I could memorize 471 girls' arm placements, toe positions, and head turns until it was my turn. Fake it till you make it? I was the living definition of it. I faked my way through pliés and pirouettes until I was one of the lucky twenty-six girls to make the team.

Now, here's when the net appeared. Through an experience only the divine could orchestrate, the legendary film director Robert Altman came to the Cowboys' ranch to film a movie starring Liv Tyler and Kate Hudson, *Dr. T and the Women*. We cheerleaders were just background in the movie, but after a couple weeks of exchanging niceties and conversation, he asked me what I wanted to do when I graduated.

I said earnestly, "I wanna be an actress; I just don't know how to do it."

He replied, "I don't know what it is, but you've got something. I think you should move to Hollywood."

Say no more, Robert! I hung up my pom-poms, quit an English major at SMU, packed up my cherry-red pickup truck, moved out west, and never looked back. My friends and family hurled their unsolicited thoughts at me like dodgeballs: "What happens if you don't make it? What's your plan B? You should work with Jean-Claude Van Damme!" I had no idea what I was getting into, but I knew one thing for sure: It didn't involve Jean-Claude.

I landed in Hollywood, settling into a humble little apartment across the street from the Pla-Boy Liquor store. I wandered the streets like some broke Baudelaire, searching for inspiration but mostly finding expired parking meters and questionable tacos. I'd lie awake at night staring at the ceiling and think, "*Shit. Was this the right move? Where's Jean-Claude?"* This was a far cry from the sleepy comfort of Euless, Texas, but I was seeking change, the way a dying man seeks water.

A couple of weeks in, I landed an audition with a manager named Daniel Rojo. My resume? So thin it might as well have been printed on a cocktail napkin. We're talking, "Lead Tree in the second-grade production of *A Christmas Carol*" thin. He asked for two monologues: one dramatic, one comedic. No big deal, right? Wrong. I walked into his office so nervous that I was convinced my heart was about to ghost me for a calmer human.

But then something wild happened. I took a deep breath, locked eyes with him, and delivered my first line. And oh. My. God. It was like I'd stepped through some kind of cosmic portal. The nerves? Gone. It felt like breathing in a forest after a rainstorm—calm, alive, electric. Like someone had wrapped me in the coziest blanket known to man. Time stopped. I was the safest and most inspired I'd ever felt. I wasn't just acting; I was home.

The net appeared yet again. George Adair famously said, "Everything you've ever wanted is on the other side of fear."

Don't stay "safe" when you could have so much more.

When Fear Is a Teacher

My kids often come to me when they're afraid, whether it's trying a new sport, meeting new friends, or standing up for themselves. I lovingly hold their hands, look them right in the eyes, and say, "Don't be afraid, you fuckin' pussy."

Can you imagine! Of course, I don't say that. But truly, the worst thing I've ever heard is when someone tells you not to be afraid ("eat low carb" is second). Who are *they* to judge where your fear factor lies? It's OK to be afraid, but walk into that fear, anyway. Speak up. Even if your voice shakes.

Fear isn't all bad. It's that primal instinct that kept us from becoming dinner for a large kitty. Sometimes, it's just your body's way of saying, "Hey, maybe set a boundary or two." But here's the thing—*you've gotta have the guts to sit with the discomfort and actually listen to what it's trying to tell you.*

You know that awful, guttural noise a dog makes before it throws up? That's exactly how I feel when I get the text: "Guess who's coming to dinner!" It's a high school friend I'd literally donate a kidney to, but when she's in a mood, she makes a hurricane look chill.

Her greatest hits?

"Why don't you homeschool your kids? Public school isn't what it used to be."

"You're still driving that car? When are you going to upgrade?"

"You should really be doing intermittent fasting. Breakfast is for amateurs."

She's a walking TED Talk on unsolicited advice, and every visit is a new episode. She's a gem, truly, but her visits leave me feeling like a soggy bag of soup. But this time, I did something different. Instead of brushing off the tension or fake-smiling my way through it, I sat with the anxiety. Let it swirl. Let it pulse. And surprise: It wasn't trying to ruin my day—it had a message. *Speak up. Even if your voice shakes.* It was pushing me towards honesty.

So, I did. Mid-visit, mid-eye-roll, after she offered me her sixth piece of "gentle" advice in under ten minutes (this one was about how my kids may never reach emotional maturity because I haven't been playing healing frequencies while they sleep), I took a deep breath and said, "I love you, but you're sucking the vibe out of this place like a Dyson on demon mode. If you can't keep your unwanted opinions to yourself, well—there's the door."

There was a long pause. The kind that makes you think, *"Should I just start packing her bags and call an Uber?"* Then she blinked, scanned the room like she was searching for backup, and said, "Oh. Okay. That's fair."

And since then…she's been better! Still a bit of a walking incense stick with opinions, but now she tries to self-regulate before launching into a full-blown spiral.

Fear taught me to speak my truth. Sometimes it's uncomfortable; sometimes you sound like you swallowed a staple, but it's worth it every time.

Growth is part of the human experience, and to stagnate is to die. We are here to experience change. To see what works. To find the magic. One step at a time. It doesn't have to be a big step, just the right-sized one that feels good at that moment. Even something as small as having the guts to try printed wallpaper in the bathroom can inspire a ripple effect of change.

The quality of your life is directly proportional to your courage. No one is coming to rescue you. That's why it's important to grow steel ovaries to *follow your truth,* even when it's messy, controversial, or means saying goodbye to people who can't handle it. Spoiler: Not everyone is meant to stick around forever, but when the shit hits the fan, are *you* going to be there for you?

Listen to that little voice within that's urging you to be more than what you already are. It's there to reconnect us with the truest, wisest, and best parts of ourselves.

No one knows what you need more than you. Bet on yourself. This is what it means to truly live with a wide-open heart that only gets bigger after it's broken. Because here's the thing: Every time your heart breaks, it doesn't get smaller; it grows. You'll get back so much more than you ever thought you lost. That's the magic of having courage.

Turn the Mirror Back on You

In the immortal words of Betty White, "Why do people say, 'Grow some balls'? Balls are weak and sensitive. If you really wanna get tough, grow a vagina. Those things really take a pounding!"

So, grow a vagina! Speak up and say what you mean, no matter what it is and no matter how small. That might look like reaching out to the person you have a crush on, telling your husband you need the night off, or breaking it to your BFF that her boyfriend gives you major "ick." What's the worst that could happen? She'll disagree? OK! Big whoop.

Grab a journal and answer the questions below, and then go out and do something about it! Don't be afraid, you fuckin' pussy. (I couldn't resist.)

1. What is it that you're most afraid to do?
2. Why are you afraid? Is it about fear of failure, rejection, stepping into the unknown?
3. Ask yourself: *What's the worst that can happen?* No, seriously—go there. Picture the absolute most dramatic, unhinged worst-case scenario. You fail. You trip onstage, spill coffee on your white shirt, accidentally reply-all to a company-wide email with a TikTok link. Now take a breath. The majority of our fears are just glittery little ghosts—loud in your head, but flimsy in real life. Ninety-nine percent of the stuff we're afraid of never actually happens. But we still hand fear the keys, letting it steer us away from the risks that might just shift our entire story. So ask yourself again: What's the worst that can happen?
4. Then ask this: What's the best? Because that version—the one where you grow, evolve, and actually surprise yourself—that's the one worth betting on.

Dating 2.0

"I went out with a guy once who told me I didn't need to drink to make myself more fun to be around. I told him, 'I'm drinking so that you're more fun to be around.'"

—CHELSEA HANDLER, THE PATRON SAINT OF SAYING WHAT WE'RE ALL THINKING

"So, what do you do for fun?"

"I'm newly single and emotionally spent. Wanna do this?"

No, no, no! Dating in your second act doesn't have to be a chore! I know you're not sixteen, and sure, you may have more mileage on your soul than on your sneakers. But congratulations! This is an exciting time! You get to start over from scratch and play by your rules now. With a little shift of your mindset, the awkward smiles, forced talk, and dumb questions can actually be fun.

This Ain't Your Grammie's Dating Scene

Take it from your favorite divorcee—swiping left and right can be daunting when the last time you dated was in the PT (pre-Tinder) era and a bit more challenging if you have roommates who call you Mom.

Yes, I know people have met their forever person on the apps, but call me old-fashioned—it wasn't for me. Too much swiping, more ghosting than there is on Halloween, and way too many hot-but-can't-spell-"definitely" types. One time, I swiped on a Warner Brothers exec thinking he might have a brain. And after he pretty much introduced himself and then said, "Wanna hang with my dick later?" I was out. Charming. Really.

Then again, dating can be a first-class ticket to Fun City should you choose to accept it. Expect to get peppered with deeply original questions like, "Do you like long walks?" But have fun with it. Answer it with something like, "Yeah to the fridge. What's your Uber rating?" This is your game, so play it however you like!

Dear reader, allow me to remind you: *You* are the main attraction. The headliner. The one they're lucky to sit across from. So why not show up as exactly who you are? Feeling flirty? Demure? Nerdy with a side of mystery? Or maybe you're leaning into unapologetically cougar-y energy? Whatever it is—own it. There are no wrong answers here. The world is your oyster, and tonight, *you're* the one holding the champagne.

And while you're out there turning heads, don't forget—you're also running a few experiments. Think of every date as a mini case study. Maybe your ex was more caveman than gentleman—grunting, not opening doors, forgetting birthdays. Well, now's your chance to gather fresh data. Try pausing by the car door and see if Mr. Swipe Right picks up the signal. This is low-stakes fieldwork, darling. You're not just dating—you're collecting evidence on what you *actually* want.

And don't stop with the dates—experiment with *you*, too. Switch up your hair, try a new lipstick, channel your inner femme fatale or awkward-cute indie heroine. It's all fair game. Bottom line? This season of dating isn't about finding someone to complete you—it's about rediscovering yourself, piece by piece, through play, curiosity, and a little lipstick. Second act? More like your *best* act.

And yes, not every date is going to be a home run. Some will be downright weird (like the guy who brings up his ex… in full-throttle detail). Some might be great but fizzle out like a fire being pissed on. Again, the key is to have fun, not take it too seriously. What do you have to lose? Even the bad ones will turn into quality entertainment at your next girls' night.

Honesty Is the Best Policy

Whether you fall in love or lust, the point is to authentically be *you*. Don't shape-shift into what you think he wants. If all he quotes is *Happy Gilmore* and you're not the beer-drinking, Adam Sandler-loving type, don't fake it to keep the vibe alive. And if you're taking it slow because you're still stitching your heart back together from the last one? Good. Take your time. But if you want to jump his bones after the first martini, by all means—just make sure it's *your* choice. The power move is showing up as your fabulous, unfiltered self—no edits, no apologizing.

And let's be clear: just because you're embracing who you are doesn't mean he can't have his moment in the spotlight. He can. But only when *you* decide to hand him the mic. You're a whole ecosystem, honey—a busy bee with things to do, places to be, and zero time to coddle a grown-ass man who emotionally shuts down all because he is not the center of your attention. If he expects to be treated like he came *out* of your vagina instead of someone trying to get *into* it—send him back to his mommy, binky and all.

I'd rather nobody like me for who I am than have a hundred people like me for who I'm not. Dating in your second act should feel empowering. We're not the insecure sluts of our twenties. We're the confident sluts of our forties! Our goal isn't to "land" a guy but to get to know ourselves more completely. *We* are the focus this time, not them.

You're not operating from doing things out of fear that he'll leave; you're operating out of your badassery, which does what it wants. *The right one will see you* and adore you for it. The Almighty One, Cher, once compared men to dessert. They're a luxury, not a necessity. So…have fun! Just don't start naming your unborn children immediately after the first date.

Turn the Mirror Back on You

I know getting out there is as scary as trying on jeans after a holiday binge, but I promise, you'll have more fun than you knew was possible if you can shift your mindset. Here are some things to think about along the way.

1. Do you miss having companionship? Or are you just looking for someone to split the guacamole bill? There are no wrong answers, but getting clear on your intention will keep you from wasting your energy.
2. What are the things you're looking for? A tall, dark, handsome drink of water with a love of travel, pets, live

music, kids, and patience (very important if you have children)? Make your wish list of your perfect partner's traits. You get a second chance at this shit, so you get to be as picky as you like! And if the person sitting across from you doesn't embody those traits, you can cut the date short. No need to waste your time being "nice." You *are* nice. You don't need to prove it.

3. Ask yourself, "What have I learned from my ex-marriage or relationship that I can apply to this next phase?" Is it to speak up? Is it to have firmer boundaries? Is it to prioritize your needs for once?
4. Don't—I repeat, don't!—bring up your ex! It's OK if you mention them lightly, but talking about them too much signals unresolved issues and just ain't sexy. First dates are about establishing chemistry and connection. If you need a therapist, find a different couch.

Divorce

"Don't waste your pretty."

—ME

As spiritual teacher, Reverend Michael Beckwith so powerfully put it, "Pain persists until the vision pulls." And for me, that vision finally pulled on an otherwise ordinary day in March 2020.

I was standing in my galley kitchen, hands trembling, tears streaming down my face at a rate that could've rivaled Niagara Falls. Not the cute, Audrey Hepburn kind of crying, either. This was a full-body unraveling—the kind that comes when you've been holding it in for too long, too tightly, for too many years. My kids were playing in their rooms, unaware that their mother was quietly setting a bomb down in the center of the life they knew. I had spent so long swallowing my needs, minimizing my pain, becoming a master of endurance. But in that moment, something snapped—and something else finally awakened.

"I want a divorce."

Four words. The air changed the second they left my lips. No screaming—just a release, like my soul had been holding its breath for years and was finally exhaling.

And then, through the wreckage of what was, I saw it—*the vision.* The one that had been whispering to me in the quiet moments between the chaos. The version of my life where I was no longer invisible. Where desire wasn't something to apologize for. Where dreams weren't luxuries—they were priorities.

Now, I knew I'd eventually pop the big question long before I actually popped it. *"Divorce?! What do you think, huh?"* Twenty years and three kids will do that—things get complicated, stretched thin, and blurry around the edges. But like the timing of a broken clock, I chose to drop the D-bomb on day one of a global lockdown. Excellent, I know.

Thanks, coronavirus! Because of you, I couldn't go out and rub up against every cute guy who crossed my path like a woman freshly reborn. Noooooo, instead, I was trapped in the house with my five-year-old twins and ten-year-old. Spiritually awakened? Sure. Emotionally raw? Very. Physically confined with three small humans and *zero* alone time? IN SPADES.

I was successfully failing at homeschooling them all, while I stared at the walls and "processed" my emotions. (I'd also like to extend my deepest gratitude to the Uber Eats driver who delivered my daily Milagro Silver by 9:10 a.m. Without you, English and geography would have been entirely impossible to get through).

This was not what I'd planned.

I wanted a VIP pass to Sin City! I always saw this moment as me parading around town like a prepubescent thirteen-year-old girl who just got her first bra! Instead, I was a slobbering, drunken mess a pint deep in Ben & Jerry's throwing Skittles at my kids' feet from under my bathroom door just to steal some alone time to cry.

The Centers for Disease Control puts the divorce rate at 3.2 per 1,000 people in the American population. Now, I've never seen a 0.2 person before, but it breaks down to something like 40 to 50 percent of marriages in America, with 70 percent of the ones filing—you guessed it—being women. But if you live in Massachusetts, buy yourself a shirt that says, "I'm better than you," because you live in the state with the lowest divorce rate of all time. Congrats bitches!

Whether you're getting a divorce or thinking of getting one, there's a lot to weigh. Don't blame yourself if you're not ready to pull the trigger. Children and moments of happiness can fool anyone into thinking, *"Maybe it'll be different this time."* The pain will persist until the vision pulls.

And trust me, pain is meant to make you grow. So grow, dear girl. It's time.

Remember Why It Happened

If you've left a marriage or are even just thinking of leaving, the very thought of not having that person in your life is like experiencing the death of a loved one. And whether you truly loved this person or you'd rather set yourself on fire than see them again, we usually romanticize their passing. All the bad shit they did is buried under our tears.

Divorce is like an emotional rubber band—you decide to leave, but then *snap*! Guilt, fear, regret, nostalgia, sadness, or the kids yank you right back. Suddenly, you're remembering all the laughter, love, sex, promises, and visions you shared, and poof—every reason the relationship didn't work magically disappears. Next thing you know, you're wailing on the couch, second-guessing yourself, watching *Eat, Pray, Love* for the seventh time, and romanticizing him like he wasn't a walking red flag.

Sister, this is when you call your girlfriends. *Immediately.* Because sometimes, you need your squad to slap some sense into you, remind you of the reality, and call your ex a loser. You may have momentary amnesia about why it didn't work, but trust me, your friends don't.

Do you keep a journal? I do, and boy was it helpful to go back and read all the pages of frustration and take a peek at those old emotions. Do yourself a favor: Go back and read your own words. It's enough to pull your head out of your ass. And if you have a mom like mine, it might be helpful to talk to her. My mom still remembers my first boyfriend back in kindergarten, who stole my Silly Putty and never gave it back—Chris, she still hasn't forgiven you.

If you have children, and you're choosing to leave, they can also serve as healthy reminders as to why the relationship is no longer serving you. After all, do you want your kids to grow up emulating your unhappy marriage? Would you want your daughter accepting behaviors that you've tolerated? Would you want your son to mimic the things he's seeing played out in front of him? As parents, we always place the needs of our children first. But what are you modeling for them by choosing to stay? Would you tell them to stay or to go if they were in a similar situation? Or would you tell them to protect their peace and choose themselves?

Now flip that mirror back on yourself.

Stop Waiting for Worse

Now, if you're waiting for the other shoe to drop in your marriage, *why*? Why do you need your situation to get even worse before you pull the plug? What's the core wound that's holding you back? Is it guilt? Do you feel guilty that you want to leave, and they don't? Sister, let me offer this: *You can be good for someone, but it doesn't mean they're good for you.* You can be a friend to someone while they are not a friend to you. Do not lower yourself to fit their standards.

If you're being plagued by guilt, get curious. Why are you putting their emotions ahead of your own? Think about the countless times you spoke up, about the things that were hurting you, the things that needed to change for you to stay—and nothing ever did.

At some point, you have to meet people where they are, not where they *could* be. Don't be with someone because of their potential. *Don't waste your pretty*. Time stops for no one.

The Only Promise Is Change

Once upon a time, I was in a relationship in which my partner looked at me wide-eyed and hopeful and said, "But aren't we going to be together forever?"

I replied softly and honestly, "I'll be here as long as I can."

It wasn't bitterness. It wasn't a lack of love. It was truth. Because no one can promise forever. But what you *can* promise is to stay as long as your spirit feels safe. As long as it feels like home. As long as you can show up as your full self without shrinking. And when that becomes no longer possible? *You're allowed to choose yourself. You matter. Your voice matters. Your peace matters. Choose you.*

If you're feeling different from how you did five, ten, fifteen years ago, that's OK. That's not a flaw. That's growth. Don't ignore it. Don't silence it to keep the peace. You're not the same person you were, and you're not meant to be. We evolve. That's what humans do. And relationships either grow *with* us—or we grow beyond them. Both outcomes are valid. Both require courage. But denying your evolution to protect someone else's comfort? Nope, your life is worth more than that.

If you're beating yourself up over ending things, remind yourself how you got here to begin with. You have to be with someone who truly loves and celebrates *all* of you—who accepts your light as well as your dark, who feels your needs are just as important as theirs. People always want the best you, but what about the worst you? Can someone accept the worst you and not punish you for it? You have to be in a relationship where you can make mistakes, learn, and grow.

Give Yourself Time and Space to Mourn

Before a caterpillar turns into a butterfly, it turns into liquid. After my divorce, I was liquid. Every day, some kind of emotion that I needed to process would come up. You can't tell when it's gonna hit you. You get some pretty weird stares when it happens over the avocados at Albertsons. Rod Stewart's "Some Guys Have All the Luck" comes on, and the next thing you know, you're throwing your body on top of the not-so-ripe ones and watering them with your tears.

Each day, sometimes each hour, will present a different emotion. Like an addict going through withdrawals, I felt a roller coaster of emotions that could hit at any place, any time, without warning. One moment, I was the saddest I'd ever been.

In another, I was feeling a bit frisky. *Hmm, does my vagina still work? Let's see… Oh. OK. Not ready for that.* I was left crying instead of climaxing with a sore hand to boot. But hey, one step at a time.

I learned to pay attention to the signals. I could be playing Monopoly with my kids, and my face would flush, my cheeks would turn red, and my eyes would swell. So, I'd breathe and just sit with it. I'd notice it. Invite it in. Ask it questions. I'd get curious about it. *Why am I feeling this way? Heart, what are you trying to tell me?*

The answer was almost always the same: guilt and sadness. Those two shadows were my companions following me even on the sunniest of days. Guilt for breaking up an almost twenty-year union and sadness for what was lost. Just like grieving the loss of a loved one, I was mourning the loss of a dream. Shock, anger, denial, guilt, bargaining, depression, acceptance—the whole emotional buffet. And guess what? It's never linear.

It doesn't necessarily get easier. It gets *different.* One day, you're fine. The next day, a song, a smell, or a stray memory can undo you. And that's OK. Emotions you thought you'd "handled" might boomerang back, demanding your attention again. So feel them all. Every single one.

My spiritual advisor (yes, I have one—I'm an actress, what did you expect? But I *draw the line* at cashew cheese. Stop lying to us—it doesn't taste like cheese) once told me, "You're crying because you're shedding your old self and birthing a new one."

So, go ahead, little caterpillar. Ugly-cry. Fall apart. Feel it all. Let yourself unravel—because that's how transformation works. You break down before you break through. And soon enough, when the dust settles and the mascara clears, it'll be time to become the butterfly.

Be Grateful and Give Your Love Back to You

But what do you do with all the love you still have for the breaker of your heart? Where does it go? You turn it toward the one person who needs it most—*you.* Pour it into yourself. Nourish yourself. Become the star of your own story. Get curious about those emotions swirling inside you. I know you want out, but the only way…is in. What are they trying to tell you? Why do they exist? When I sat with my heartache—no running, no numbing—I started to understand myself in ways I never had before. Like, "Oh, so this is why I let that slide," or "Here's what really lights me up." It wasn't easy—it was ugly-cry-on-the-bathroom-floor hard—but that's how I learned my boundaries, what I needed to work on, and what made me feel truly alive.

And here's the twist—I was grateful for the ache. Yup, that's right. Because it's brave to love so deeply that it breaks you. I could be proud of *how* I loved. My love is big. It's mad. It's wild. My love has wings. I loved like I've never been hurt. But sometimes, love isn't enough. And the fallout is this vulnerable, chaotic fragility that needs to be looked after—and if you have the courage to be still and listen, you will learn about yourself in ways you never have before.

As the king of romantic pain himself, Nicholas Sparks, wrote, "The emotion that can break your heart is sometimes the very one that heals it." I didn't truly understand the strength of my own heart until my divorce. It broke me, yes, but it also rebuilt me.

I didn't need anyone else to save me—I was my own damn life raft. I started to trust myself. My heart had been broken many times, and each time, as painful as it was, it had the courage to put itself back together. That's the magic of a human heart—it's not just strong; it's indestructible.

So don't you dare underestimate your power, sister. You're fucking incredible. You've got everything you need to heal already inside you. Trust yourself. Love yourself. And when your heart is ready, it'll surprise you with how brave it truly is. So, dive headfirst into yourself and be thankful you've got a seat at your soul's table.

No Regrets

When we walk away from someone, we don't do it to teach them a lesson but because we finally learned ours. And if someone walked away from you, thank them, because they opened the door for someone else who is more in vibration with who you truly are.

As Maya Angelou said, "People who know better, do better," and believe it or not, you both did the best you could. You can spend ten more years of your pretty trying to contort yourself into the version of the woman who would fit the marriage, or you can face facts—you're both amazing, but the marriage? It's just not the goose that lays the golden egg anymore.

It takes real guts to say, "This isn't about you or me. You're the bee's knees, I'm the cat's pajamas, but this dance? It's out of step. It's not serving *us.*" That's not throwing in the towel—that's knowing when to cut your losses and start fresh

I don't regret anything. And knowing those eighteen years gave me three wonderful children, I'd do it all over again. Life's too short to sit on your hands waiting for things to change. Sometimes, you've gotta grab the bull by the horns, let bygones be bygones, and turn over a new leaf. You deserve your dream life, not some budget version you settle for.

So put on your big-girl pants, grab the wheel, and go get it. Because this life of yours? It's all yours to build. And honestly, who better to make it amazing than you? Get a fresh cut, shake it off, and strut into your next chapter like the boss you are.

Turn the Mirror Back on You

If you're in a place where you're thinking about leaving, start with where you are, and be very patient with yourself. Think on the following questions:

1. What are the top hits of your marital problems? And what are you *not* experiencing that you want to? What part of this is yours to clean up? Most important, have you done everything you can do to save the marriage? Therapy, date nights, love languages? If you end up leaving, at least you know you gave it your all. Because let me tell you, dividing assets, sucks ass.
2. What might your life look like without the other person? Maybe it's footing your own bills or as blissful as coming home to actual peace and quiet. Maybe it's swapping the big house for a chic little apartment or finally saying yes to that dog you've been secretly obsessed with. Who might you become outside of this marriage? Without the weight of compromise or the constant negotiations, who are you when you're just…you?

3. Now, what would happen if you decided to stay? More fights? Not being happy? Promises that keep getting broken? Invite the feelings in as you write it all down.
4. And if you're the one who was left behind—if you didn't choose this ending—know this: it might feel like you've been sentenced to the DMV of heartbreak while everyone else is out winning the lottery. But trust me, this is your turning point too. You've been handed a blank page. So write it your way. Who are you blossoming into when no one's expectations are weighing you down? Make it spicy. Make it bold. This is still your show—and you get to rewrite the whole script. One day, you may even look back and realize this heartbreak was the greatest gift you never asked for. But until then, give yourself grace. You're allowed to be both undone and unstoppable.

Ego: Friend and Foe

"I once thought about being humble, and then I realized no one would notice unless I told them."

—ATTRIBUTED TO FRAN LEBOWITZ, ICONIC WRITER AND SELF-DESCRIBED "SLACKER ICON"

I used to think the ego was that sassy little voice inside saying, "Step aside, everyone. I'm not saying I'm better than you, but I'm saying I'm better than you. And btw, isn't it distracting how beautiful my eyes are?" Reverend Michael Beckwith describes the ego as "E.G.O," or "edging God out." Ego is a belief that separates us from our higher self, God, the Guardian of the Galaxy, the Universe, the Mother Lode, or whatever you call it.

But contrary to what you've been told, it doesn't completely suck. Though its main job is to keep you rooted in your shadow self—the part that is anxious, fearful, and operates out of a lack of self-worth—if you dig a little deeper, you'll see that all it really wants is to protect you. You know, like your well-intentioned Albanian auntie who doesn't want you to take any swinging hits at life for fear of failure and keeps feeding you plates of cookies because "you deserve it." She will beat you over the head trying to keep you "safe" from doing anything outside of your normal routine—because she just wants to make sure you're loved, plump, and happy!

The key here is to appreciate your ego's role without letting it take the driver's seat on your journey.

Mr. New Nuts Brought New Thoughts

When the world finally reopened, I emerged with a post-divorce strut that said, "You missed me, didn't you?" I was a huge fan of the afternoon date because it wasn't as long as the dinner date, and I could still be home by five to be with my kids. My afternoon date uniform? Yoga pants and a half shirt that read "Wine Not." I also signed all my receipts with a heart. Yuck.

A lot of guys were a solid "meh," but one guy in particular made everyone else sound like background noise. He was hot, had a great job, a child of his own, and totally bangable. The date ended on a high note with the promise that he'd call me later that night.

EEEEEKKK! My first love connection post-divorce! I felt like a lovestruck teen. I put the kids down earlier than normal and waited for him to call. And waited and waited…and waited.

Cue the ego!

"Hold on a second, Mr. New Nuts—don't you know how lucky you are to even have my number? I'm hot and funny, and you won't do any better than me."

I started spiraling: *He doesn't like me, maybe I shouldn't have worn that shirt, did I talk about our hypothetical children too much?*

I rang him up, pretending to be distracted while I left him a message. "Oh, hi, Greg, sorry…hold on a sec, there's someone at the door (that'll make him think I'm a hot-ticket item—EGO!)…OK, I'm back. Whatever. Call me."

He didn't. Days went by, and naturally, I did what any normal girl would do—I went all CSI on Instagram. He could post a pic of himself at brunch, but not call me back? The nerve (ego)! Time to dial my emergency support system, Michelle.

> Michelle: "He doesn't owe you a call just because you had coffee. That's your ego speaking right there. He has the right to change his mind. Maybe he's not that into you after all?"
>
> Me (bursting into tears): "Of course he was into me! He liked my shirt!"
>
> Michelle: "He may have liked your socks too, but that doesn't mean he likes *you*. And why are you crying? You don't even know him!"
>
> Me: "But he laughed at my jokes!"
>
> Michelle: "Who cares! Maybe he met his future wife right after meeting you? Or he lost his phone. Maybe he got into a car crash and lost his memory! It doesn't matter. The point is, why are you giving this guy so much power? Do you think he's the last guy on earth who will want to have coffee with you?"

Needless to say, Michelle had her work cut out for her that night. But she was right. Somewhere between the third tissue and the fourth glass of wine, I got to thinking: *Why am I wasting tears on some guy I just met? That's not like me.*

I took a deeper look into my hurt feelings to see what I was reacting to because it surely wasn't about Mr. New Nuts. What I found was a tangled mess of not feeling like I was good enough for someone to love, unresolved divorce trauma, and at the heart of it all, some age-old abandonment woes, courtesy of dear old Dad.

After clocking a lot of hours in therapy and with Michelle, it hit me like the ending of a good rom-com. You know, the part where the lead finally sees herself clearly and usually in great lighting—*I am enough, I am lovable, and the only person who truly has the power to abandon me is me.*

I also realized: If he can't dial, don't waste a smile.

You are the MVP of Your Love Story

Listen, homie, you *are* love. You came straight from that infinite source in the sky—the one that's pure, unfiltered, star-level love. Literally, the same force that created galaxies and sunsets decided, *You know what this world needs? You.*

So stop looking around for someone else to stamp your greatness with approval. You don't need exterior validation to prove how incredible you are—it's already built in! Your only job is to recognize it, own it, and bask in your brilliance. That's *your* job. Not anyone else's.

Your ego isn't trying to sabotage you; trying to get rid of it is like asking a politician to tell the truth. IT WON'T HAPPEN. But if you dig a little deeper, you'll see it's actually trying to help you uncover what you need. Make friends with your ego, invite it in, and listen to what it's really saying.

Acts of Service or Acts of War

So, let's say your love language is *acts of service.* Then your partner taking out the trash is basically foreplay. But when they casually stroll past an overflowing bin like it's some kind of modern art installation, it can feel personal.

The gloves are off and your ego kicks in fast: *"He doesn't respect me! Does he think I'm the maid? Am I just here to clean up after him?"* But if you take a breath and listen a little closer, your ego is actually whispering something softer: *"I want to feel like we're a team. I want to know he's got my back."* It's not really about the trash—it's about feeling seen, supported, and appreciated. So instead of launching into a monologue about the sacred symbolism of garbage duty, try something lighter: a loving reminder that taking out the trash equals instant brownie points. And hey—maybe next time he'll do it without being asked.

Picture this: You dropped half your paycheck at the salon, walked out looking like a goddess, and floated home expecting your partner to gasp in awe. Instead, he squints and says, "Did you do something different?" Yes, Chad, I got a *whole new life*. Thanks for your Pulitzer-worthy observation. Now you're fuming, plotting his demise, and googling "how to hide a body without getting caught."

But when you sit down and have a heart-to-heart with your ego, you realize it's not about the haircut. It's about feeling unseen. Your ego's over there waving a little flag like, "Hello! Can we get some acknowledgment here? Maybe a compliment that took more than half a second of effort?" What you really want isn't a full-blown sonnet about your hair—it's to feel valued, noticed, and cherished. Turns out, the ego is just looking out for your heart. Hit him with a grin and say, "Come on, don't make me fish for it—how good do I look?"

The Danger Zone

However, it's important to tell the difference between the small stuff and the big stuff. Like, is it just that he keeps watching your favorite shows without you? Annoying, yes, but not the end of the world. (Although if he spoils the season finale one more time, he's sleeping on the couch.)

But then there's the big stuff—like when he never acknowledges you or shows any appreciation. That's not just hurt feelings; that's a "Houston, we have a problem" situation. One is a slap on the wrist; the other is a full-on intervention.

Pick your battles wisely. Sometimes it's Netflix betrayal; sometimes it's needing to feel seen and loved. And sometimes, you're just hangry—so maybe have a snack first before deciding which hill to die on. Take it all in as information. When you attune your antennae to the quieter needs of your soul, you can have a healthy relationship with your ego. After all, all it wants is your attention.

Turn the Mirror Back on You

Your ego: You can't live with it, and you really can't live without it. It serves a great purpose in regulating your survival, but you can't let it run the show.

1. Kill the need to be liked by everyone. Not everyone's going to vibe with you, and that's fine—you're not

meant to be everyone's cup of tea. As long as you like you, you're golden.

2. The ego's like a spoiled toddler—it wants attention, compliments, gifts, and freaks out when it doesn't get them. The fix? Flip the script. Give instead of take. Go serve a Thanksgiving meal at a shelter and watch your ego vanish faster than leftover pie.
3. Your ego's roots likely go all the way back to some childhood wound. Take a quiet moment to ask yourself: *When was the first time I felt unloved or ignored?* That little girl inside you—the one still carrying that pain—needs to hear that she's loved. So tell her. Because here's the truth: You're made of star stuff, a literal spark of the universe. The love you've been searching for? It's been within you all along.

Enthusiasm

"Passion is energy. Feel the power that comes from focusing on what excites you."

—THE BOSS OF PERSONAL GROWTH, OPRAH WINFREY

I want you to tackle the shit out of enthusiasm. That's right! Be a motherfucker for your own joy. We're all so quick to vent about our problems, but what about venting over the things that make us *happy*?

We notoriously walk through life bitching about everything that goes wrong. Like network news, we spew out negative story after story, but then wonder why our lives are in such a funk. "Well, I woke up late today, Johnny has a cold, I didn't get the promotion after all, and Ted forgot to unload the dishwasher *again*!"

Next day: "Ugh, I slept like shit, there's a leak under the faucet, my one o'clock lunch canceled, I forgot to make the cookies for the bake sale, and Max took a shit on my rug." In this scenario, Max could be a dog or a toddler. Your choice. (You have a serious problem if he's an adult.)

Shit happens, and we need a sounding board to preserve our sanity. But if it's that easy to bitch about the things that make us miserable, why don't we "bitch" about the things that bring us joy? Who cares about staying cool and level-headed? Also, it's pretty damn righteous that you don't need big moments in order to rejoice. You just need to pay attention.

Marvel at all the little things, like all the kids getting in the car on time in the morning, a delicious meal, a great parking spot, or the sound of a crackling fire. As soon as you do this, it'll start coming out of your pores. It'll even creep into your conversations that were once mostly about misery loving company. "I had the greatest sleep ever. My therapy session was awesome. My husband really came through with dinner tonight." Be over the top with that shit. It feels soooo good not to focus on Max shitting on your rug!

When you find something that floats your boat, geek out over it. Be so enthusiastic, it's silly. I start off every morning with a cup of coffee, black. With just the first sip, my tastebuds giggle with excitement, and I tell myself, "This is the best cup of coffee I've ever had." It doesn't matter if I have the same delicious cup tomorrow! I feel this way right now! Sister, I want you to be obnoxious about the things you believe in. Allow yourself to feel it in your bones. When you're excited about something, not only are you injecting the most positive vibes into the situation, but you're also inspiring others to throw some gusto at it as well. And you are what you attract, so you'll only attract even more situations to be enthusiastic about. It's quite literally contagious!

Be it a project at work or in your personal life, if you choose to engage in anything, don't hold back or half-ass it! I can tell you right now you're better than lukewarm. *Give life your all.*

Enthusiasm is the ingredient that turns the ordinary into magic. The beauty of life is that we get to choose how we react to the cards in front of us. Participate in your life with the utmost joy because what's the alternative? As Charles Bukowski noted, "Find what you love and let it kill you."

Turn the Mirror Back on You

The word "enthusiasm" literally comes from the Greek for being "inspired or possessed by a god." Not too shabby of an emotion to have! Here are some things to think about if you're having trouble finding your excitement.

1. Make a list of the things you love and do one of them every day. It can be as simple as cooking, growing basil on your windowsill, blasting your music in the car, or going for walks. The more joy you inject in your heart, the more excitement you'll naturally find.
2. Stop playing small! Geek out over the little things in front of you. If all you've got going on are the school pickups and drop-offs, I challenge you to be *extra* when doing them. Make it the best it can be. Smile from ear to ear while telling your kids this is the best day ever. It's contagious! They'll feel it, too.
3. Shake up your daily routine. How the fuck are you supposed to get excited about something you can do with your eyes closed? Bor-ing! Go left instead of right. Do your grocery shopping at a different store. Have dinner outside.

4. Be the host. If Jessica always throws game nights at her house, why don't you offer to do the next one? Or host a girls' wine night. Doing something you usually don't do and seeing it through will add some extra sparkle to your heart.

Failure and Fucking Up

"You yourself, as much as anybody in the entire universe, deserve your love and affection."

—BUDDHA, THE O.G. CHILL INFLUENCER WAY BEFORE INFLUENCING WAS EVEN A THING

As an Aries rising (which basically means I act now, think later...a lot), my epitaph should read, "Here lies a woman who looked at life and thought, 'I probably shouldn't, but I'll do it anyway.'" Let's be real here, buttercup—no good story ever started with, "So...I was out with this really hot guy last night annnddd...I had too much... salad." Nope. More like, "So...I was out with this really hot guy last night annddd...there was a lot of tequila and zero regrets. At least for the first two hours."

This part of my personality has led to some impulsive shit that has really worked out for me, and other times, some impulsive shit that I *thought* would work out for me. Either way, life is going to throw some punches. Sometimes I duck; sometimes I just take it to the face and call it exfoliation. Life is lifey and it's not about how we fall, but how we pick ourselves up after.

An Affair to Remember

It was 1999. I was all of nineteen years old, a full-time student at Southern Methodist University and a full-time cheerleader for the Dallas Cowboys (cover girl for the year 2000 right here). Dear reader, if you've ever been to Texas, you know the only thing they love more than God is football—and with that, the cheerleaders are hailed as the greatest thing since Nutella. Yes, I was hot shit.

I also had Paul #1 (his name was not actually Paul #1, but all my boyfriends in this chapter will numerically be named Paul), my sweet, innocent, never-pressured-me-to-have-sex, full-time high school boyfriend who became my full-time college boyfriend, who still never pressured me to do anything other than dry humping.

However, unbeknownst to Paul #1, our relationship went into the part-time bucket once I shifted into newfound maturity.

But I Couldn't Not Be into Him

While I was still with Paul #1, I met Paul #2 at Johnnie High's Country Music Revue in Arlington, Texas—a weekly variety show showcasing unknown talent and up-and-comers. He was the up-and-comer; I was the unknown. He was a tall drink of water with Elvis-level swagger—handsome, confident, and a voice so smooth it could tame a lion. Oh, and did I mention he was ten years older and drove a fast car? Compared to him, Paul #1 might as well have still been in diapers.

I was backstage waiting for my turn to go on, all bedazzled in my jeweled bustier and cowboy hat, when Paul #2 struck up a conversation. After a couple bashful exchanges and a little wink, I was besotted. After the show, we walked out to our cars, exchanged numbers, and then…he kissed me.

Panty drop.

My nineteen-year-old self was left dizzy and dazed. We started seeing each other, and I would sneak him into my dorm room on Fridays when the RA fucked off. I delivered any lie imaginable to Paul #1 in order to see Paul #2: "I'm tired; I have too much homework; I have lice." I said things a girl would never say to the boy she was dating: "I have to go to the store to buy super tampons. My period is *very* heavy."

The weeks turned into months, and the next thing I knew, I was having an affair. Brand me with a bright-red A on my chest. I was now like Demi Moore in *The Scarlet Letter*, all heaving bosom and adultery.

Now, growing up in the South, I judged the shit out of people who cheated on their significant others. I didn't care if all you did was hold Malcom's hand in kindergarten while you were betrothed to James—you were James's girl, and you better drop Malcom's hand now!

But then came Paul #2, and suddenly, my moral high ground was sinking like quicksand. Like with chocolate, my resistance was futile. My conscience kicked me the entire time. I had to drink about five shots of liquid courage every time I saw him just to quiet that bitch down: "You're a cowardly cunt. Tell Paul #1 your feelings have changed! But this is so fun. Paul #2 is so hot. He's sophisticated and I deserve that. I won't get caught!" It was a full-on internal circus, and every time the night ended, I'd wake up the next morning feeling disgusted and furious with myself. But also…

I couldn't wait to see him again.

Caught Red-Handed

After about two months of "heavy periods and a recurring bout of lice," Paul #1 started suspecting something was off. One Saturday night, we had made plans to go to dinner and see a movie. Being the deceptive dick that I was, I canceled last minute due to a "stomachache" and decided to meet up with Paul #2 instead. Unlike other times, Paul #1 didn't complain about me canceling. He was remarkably understanding. I thought that meant I was in the clear. Nope. Mud was clearer.

I was grinding up against Paul #2 at the Lizard Lounge downtown when I locked eyes with Paul #1 staring at me. The blood rushed from my face, and I gawked back at him like he was a ghost. He ran out; I ran out after him. We both knew the relationship was done. It was evident. I no longer carried the same feelings for him as I did in high school. But it was also evident I was a lying ball of dick cheese for not telling him.

Paul #2 and I never saw each other again after that night. He went off to pursue his career, and I was yesterday's news. I couldn't stop beating myself up. Not for the relationship with Paul #1 ending but for *how* it ended. Yes, I hurt him, yes, I betrayed him, but the person I betrayed the most was me.

Why couldn't I have just told him the truth? Why couldn't I have faced him like the honest person I *thought* I was? I'd always prided myself on being better than that—better than secrets, better than sneaking around, better than hiding behind lies. But now, I wasn't. I had stooped so low, and I couldn't forgive myself for it. I felt worthless.

The shame spiral was real and unrelenting. I became a part-time bulimic, stuffing my feelings down with food only to force them back up later. I drank too much, numbing myself to the self-loathing that wouldn't leave me alone. I pulled away from everyone becoming a ghost of myself. And the worst part? I felt like I deserved it. I had to pay for my mistakes.

Own Your Oops

After a year of feeling like a total disaster, I finally bit the bullet and went to therapy. Between that and binge-watching hours of Tony Robbins videos, I learned step one of self-forgiveness: acceptance. I had to let go. Fighting my mistakes was like swimming upstream in jeans—it was exhausting, and I was getting nowhere. I had to accept what I did, accept that I'm human, and accept that mistakes are part of the package. Some are tiny; some are as big as the sky. But they're mine.

Here's what I learned: *I'm not my mistakes.* Up until then, I had myself pegged as pond scum, full-on bottom-feeder vibes like I was a mustache-twirling villain plotting world heartbreak. But what about the rest of me? I'm a great daughter, a solid sister, a hard worker, and someone who genuinely cares about others. I'm ambitious, I'm smart, and yeah, I screw up sometimes. If I'm going to slap a label on myself, shouldn't it at least be an accurate one?

Newsflash: You're allowed to be both flawed and fabulous. It's called being human. And that's when I finally saw the light at the end of the tunnel: self-compassion.

I was just a flawed, messy human who made a choice, tried something new, and learned the hard way that it made me feel like dog shit. Whether I use that lesson to do better moving forward? *That's on me.* If I *choose* to stay fucked up over it? *That's on me.*

The mistakes taught me lessons I couldn't have learned any other way. Honestly, without those screw-ups, I wouldn't be this locked into my morals now. And trust me, post-Paul #1 and Paul #2, I became a human "no cheating zone." Once I was in a relationship, every other guy became a Ken doll to me—no genitals and zero appeal. If I'm taken, I'm taken.

Moral of the story: Mistakes don't define you, but how you grow from them? That's the real glow-up.

The Art of the Bounce Back

Peanut, you're going to mess up. Big whoop! We're all granted the glorious, messy privilege of screwing up and learning from it. And who decided there's a "right" way to learn anyway?

Your life is yours, and your mistakes? They're tailor-made for you. Call them lessons, plot twists, or life's way of giving you a crash course in being human. So you bombed the pop quiz? Who cares? Dust yourself off, take the lesson, and keep moving. Judging yourself for failing is like judging a cloud for being too fluffy. It's ridiculous. There's no "wrong"—just different paths to figuring it out.

Your job? To show up ferociously as you in every single moment and trust that it's all unfolding for a reason bigger than you can see right now. If something feels good, roll with it. If it feels like a bag of regret, congratulations—you've just learned it's not for you. Don't shrink your sparkle just because of a mistake. It's your beautiful, wild life—own it.

Turn the Mirror Back on You

OK, so you feel like a bag of garbage because you did something you wish you hadn't. Trust me, you deserve to move on. You were not put on this planet to harbor guilt, so embrace your fuck-ups by doing the following:

1. Apologize. You are not less of a person for admitting your mistake. If anything, it shows your strength. Take ownership of what happened and its effects.
2. Think of this as a plot twist, not a failure. Every "oops" is a chance to become even better than you were before. The universe hasn't canceled you, so don't cancel yourself. If self-love feels hard right now, start small—affirmations, journaling, whatever works.
3. And here's the big one: Ask yourself why. Were you feeling unloved? Unhappy? Maybe you were outgrowing something but too scared to admit it? Face the stuff you've been dodging. You're stronger than you realize. Own your shit, learn from it, and keep moving. You're the main character in this story—don't forget that.

Follow Your Happy

"Just because you're in a puddle doesn't mean you can't splash."

—ME. OR MAYBE A COCKTAIL NAPKIN. BUT CUTE, RIGHT?

I was knee-deep in my first dark night of the soul (there have been a few—Aries rising, remember? Drama is basically my cardio) when I stumbled on Goldie Hawn's episode of *Super Soul Sunday*. She was spilling tea about how she became an actor, and surprise: It wasn't some master plan. She was a dancer with dreams of a cozy little life—get married, open a dance studio, live happily ever after.

One day, a talent agent caught one of her performances and thought she was as cute as a bug in a movie trailer. He handed her his card and told her to come in and audition for him. And what did Goldie do on the big day? She forgot! She was so caught up doing whatever lit her up in that moment—probably dancing, laughing, or just being an absolute ray of chaotic sunshine—that the audition totally slipped her mind. She dropped the ball so hard, it bounced into another time zone and possibly knocked over a cactus on its way out.

But her blissful oblivion didn't turn the agent off—it hooked him even harder. He was drawn to the unfiltered joy, the authenticity, the "this-is-me-whether-you're-watching-or-not" energy. It wasn't a calculated move; she was just too busy chasing whatever made her happiest in each moment. No ego. No strategy board with a five-year plan. Just a woman so tuned in to following her joy that it radiated off her like perfume.

So if it worked for Goldie? That free-spirited, bliss-chasing, light-hearted magic? It's good enough for me. *Follow your happy.* The rest will find you.

Booty Calls from Life

In my line of work, job security is about as dependable as your ex's texting habits—completely nonexistent. I hit a dry spell so bad, I didn't see a dime of income for almost two years. I was circling the drain in spectacular, pear-shaped fashion.

I threw myself at every casting director in town, auditioning for roles I had *no business* even thinking about. Sixty-five-year-old white woman? No problem! That's about as easy as putting lipstick on a pig. I was so far down in the dumps, calling me "miserable" would've been a compliment.

Then one day, exhausted from all the hustling and rejection, I threw my hands up and yelled, "Alright, universe, you win! You want me broke and jobless? Fine. I'll just be over here eating ramen and having meaningful conversations with my plants!"

With nothing left to lose, I stopped pouring my energy into chasing things that were never meant for me. Instead, I redirected it toward things that actually made me *happy*. I stopped cold-calling casting directors and started hosting game nights with my friends. I stopped auditioning for roles that were wrong for me and started volunteering at my kids' schools. I went for long, winding drives, blasting everything from country music to classic rock just because I could. I painted my nails wild colors I'd never usually wear. I followed *my* happy.

Two months later, I booked *Sex/Life*.

When life hits us with a booty call—because ya know, it wants to keep fucking us over—we feel like a grade A loser. And what do we do? We put all our energy into making it stop. But you can't stop life's bullshit any more than you can stop the rain. So quit wasting your energy fighting the struggle.

Now, it's a primal law of the universe that whatever you focus on grows. Obsessing over the crappy stuff? That's just like watering weeds. It blocks the epic things that are *literally* waiting for you. And this isn't about slapping on fake positivity or gaslighting yourself into being "fine." Negative emotions are totally normal. They're not your enemy; they're like little internal text messages saying, "Hey, something's off—pay attention." They're not the whole story, just one piece of the puzzle.

So, what do you do? Change your focus. Stop wrestling with the struggle and follow your happy. Whatever adds a skip to your step, do *that.* Go for a walk. Blast your favorite song and have a dance break in the kitchen. Watch a movie that makes you laugh-cry. Try on lipstick you don't need at CVS. Play bingo with your kids and take 'em for everything they've got. When you focus on the stuff that lights you up, you'll find your next steps practically waving at you like, *"Hey, gorgeous, this way!"*

That's when everything shifts. When you stop chasing every squirrel in your brain and just do what feels good, life starts connecting the dots for you. That's the magic. You don't figure out the next move by overthinking it; you find it by living it. Pivot, find your joy, and let the rest work itself out. Goldie knew it, I've learned it, and now, so will you.

Turn the Mirror Back on You

One baby step at a time, just do what makes you feel good, and the next step you're supposed to take will come knocking at your door. What's meant for you will always find you.

1. What makes you happy? Don't think too hard. Write down the first things that come to mind. A ripe avocado. Perfectly glazed donuts. Reruns of your fave '80s sitcom. A good hair day. Your dog. Your boobs. Making people laugh. That list will tell you volumes about where you can naturally shift focus if you want to smile more often.
2. Even when rock bottom is calling your name, it's easier to take steps towards your happy when you come from a place of gratitude. Miracles are happening all around you, but most of the time, you're too busy wallowing in your cup of sorrow to take note. Even the small things can get you to feel the big feelings. Being in gratitude is the fast track to awesomeness. The more you practice it, the more awesome things you'll experience. It's the best catch-22 there is.
3. Don't overthink it. Following your happy can be as simple as ordering the burger instead of the salad because that's what you *actually* want. Or skipping girls' night

to take a solo walk on the beach because that's what your soul needs. Step by step, choice by choice, you end up exactly where you're meant to be.

Gas-Station Fashion

"I don't dress for the occasion. I am the occasion."

—YOURS TRULY

Hi, my name is Sarah, and I'm an addict. My drug of choice? Comfort. Lawd, lawd, lawd have mercy...I don't give a shit if my socks are mismatched or I'm wearing Christmas pajamas in July. I wear my truth like a badge of honor, and when it comes to my everyday look, I wear whatever I feel the most comfortable in. The majority of the time, my clothes look like they came from the 76 on a road trip from California to New Mexico. Hence, my kids have dubbed it *gas-station fashion*.

You know what I'm talking about, baby! The oversized, faded-blue Harley T-shirt with an eagle on it, or a floppy velvet cowboy hat with a fake feather sticking out. Style is personal and is meant to reflect whatever mood we're in. Most of the time,

I'm in a "half- boho-burnout- half couch-gremlin" mood. But I look at clothes as an extension of how we present ourselves. You can be as outlandish or basic as you like, but the key is to dress for *you*. When you stop caring what other people think, you are free to be you. The *real* you. The you on the inside.

I wasn't always like this. Like many women, I would practically kill myself trying to stay on trend by squeezing into clothes that were two sizes too small, mostly to impress some loser who didn't even own a passport and called a six-pack a six-course meal. I spent the majority of my twenties tying dental floss around my waist and calling it a skirt, or fastening a handkerchief around my tits and calling it a shirt.

Have I been known to go back to that style every now and then? Absolutely! But the difference is that *now* I do it for *me.* I've learned that when I dress in accordance with how I feel, I own the truth of who I am in that moment, which always creates a better outcome. Be it in a meeting with a creative executive, an audition, or racing around the grocery store, I have a better time when I'm dressed how I want. Rockstar, gypsy, sex kitten, bum on the corner of the interstate—they all live inside me, and I allow each of them to take center stage when I feel it. Dressing for *myself* is the ultimate power move, and it's the only trend I'll ever follow again.

Wear Your Inside on Your Outside

August 2009: I'd just given birth to my first son, Wolf, when I got an audition for a new USA Network show called *Fairly Legal*, for the lead, Kate Reed, a lawyer who hates lawyers.

A lawyer? As in the kind that wears power suits? Big problem.

I was twenty pounds heavier, sleep-deprived, and rocking Vienna-sausage vibes in anything tailored. There was no way I was squeezing into a power suit, so I threw on the next best thing—bright orange Nike shorts, the baggiest white tee I could find, and a blazer. Nothing says hot-shot attorney like gym shorts and an oversized tee.

But as I left for the audition, there was one glaring issue: I forgot to pump. Rookie mom mistake. You know that tingly feeling you get when your boobs are filling with milk? The "letdown"? Yup, that happened. Mid-audition. My milk let down—through my bra, onto my oversized tee, in front of eight network execs. And we're not talking a dainty little drip. It was like a busted keg at a frat party. Mortified, I powered through, using my embarrassment to fuel the scene and bolted for the door as soon as I hit the last line.

An hour later, my agent called: "They loved you! That messy energy is perfect for the character." Turns out, leaky boobs, baggy tees, and not giving a damn were the exact vibes Kate Reed needed. Go figure.

The moral of the story? Dressing for *you* is a power move. Not just any power—*internal power.* The kind no one can take away from you. It's not about how you look; it's about how you *feel.* When you feel good in what you're wearing, you're unstoppable. So, toss the heels that make your feet look like loaves of baked bread and forget what's "expected." This is about *you.* If Serena Williams can strut into the Met Gala in sneakers, you can rock whatever the hell makes you feel like the main character anywhere and everywhere.

Dressing for yourself isn't just about style—it's about owning your moment, whatever that looks like. And sometimes that moment is milk-soaked and still winning.

And PS: Keds for life. The dirtier, the better. Forever a '90s girl.

Turn the Mirror Back on You

If squeezing into an outfit like a sardine makes you feel confident, do it. If you're vibing with the toga life and want to rock a bedsheet, have at it. Who cares what that random stranger over there thinks? A $3,000 Balenciaga jacket isn't going to make people like you any more than a $30 Target one. Wear what makes you feel unstoppable—end of story.

1. How would you dress if you could wear whatever you wanted at any point in the day? Would you wear PJs to work? Sneakers to dinner? Find a way to do you always. Be a rebel and dress against the occasion sometimes.
2. If you feel like you can't wear your true self on your sleeve, are you afraid you won't be liked? If someone likes or dislikes you based on what you wear, how superficial is that? Look up Rick Rubin or the famed director Julian Schnabel. They're both incredibly powerful, respected men who wear PJs during public appearances. Why? *Because they*

Illustration by Violet Howey

feel like it. It's what's on the inside that you're presenting to the world, not what's on the outside.

3. Do you have body issues? Yes…*and*??? So does everyone else! Everyone puts their pants on one leg at a time; I don't care what their body looks like! Who gives a fuck? Do you, sister. Who knows? Maybe you'll even inspire people to tap into their playful side, all because you wore a green wig, sailor cap, torn fishnets, '90s Doc Martens, and heart-shaped glasses.

Grace over Grudges

"When you forgive, you in no way change the past—but you sure do change the future."

—BERNARD MELTZER, THE OG ADVICE GURU OF TALK RADIO

I used to think forgiveness meant rolling out the red carpet for the person who hurt me, letting them waltz back into my life while I prayed to literally every deity I'd ever heard of—God, Krishna, Beyoncé, Thanos—that they wouldn't screw me over again. It always felt like a crapshoot and as fate would have it, my odds would've been better in Vegas.

But after a lifetime of therapy, surviving a drug-addict dad, failed relationships, broken friendships, three kids, a divorce, and a career in La La Land, I finally had a software upgrade in my brain.

Forgiveness isn't about forgetting what happened or handing out a free pass to someone who acted like a jackass. It's not about saying, "Oh, it's fine!" when it absolutely wasn't. Forgiveness is for *you.* It's an act of grace you give yourself to break free from the emotional merry-go-round of resentment. It's not tidy or fast. It's messy; it's slow; and sometimes it feels as awkward as trying to clean peanut butter off a spoon with one hand. But in the end, forgiveness isn't about them—it's about setting *yourself* free.

But I Don't Want to Forgive

Well, as karma loves a good plot twist, payback for my college affair came gift-wrapped as Paul #3, my first love in LA. Paul was an aspiring comedian (emphasis on aspiring) who cheated on me with an equally aspiring (double emphasis on aspiring) erotic model for car magazines. They met at a boozy car show in LA, and one night while I was at his house, a mysterious hair tie and a different brand of tampon made it pretty clear he was revving someone else's engine. Classic. It felt like fate drop-kicked me right in the panties. Now I knew exactly how Paul #1 felt. But I chose to stay with my lame comedian, tagging along to his even lamer shows—because what can I say? The heart wants what it wants, and at the time, it hurt more to leave than to stay.

But forgive him? Hell no! I thought it made me weak, like I was sweeping his affair under the rug. Instead, I cradled my anger like it was my emotional support animal, giving him death stares so cold they could freeze lava. As long as I stayed mad, I felt like I had the upper hand. His betrayal fueled me, and honestly, it felt good knowing he felt bad.

He showed great remorse, beat himself up daily, showered me with constant praise, changed his number, and even offered to let me see his phone whenever I wanted. While most would have jumped at this offer to see if Little Miss would reach out, what would I have turned into if I suspiciously grabbed his phone every time he set it down?

After months, my resentment became all too heavy for me to carry. And as Cheryl Strayed, the author who can poetically turn life's dumpster fires into soul-filled journeys, so wisely said, "Forgiveness doesn't sit there like a pretty boy in a bar. Forgiveness is the old fat guy you have to haul up a hill." It's tougher than a two-dollar steak to forgive the person who caused you pain, but I either had to choose to forgive or choose to move the fuck on.

It took a massive amount of communication, tears, new agreements regarding his drinking, and a giant leap of faith, but I moved forward with the relationship, and came out wiser than before. Since he'd now shown me this side of himself, if he was a repeat offender, it would be *chosen* behavior, and I'd be gone quicker than the whiskey sliding down his throat.

A year later, Paul #3 cheated on me again—shocking, I know—and that was my cue to leave. At this point, being mad at him felt like wasted energy. He'd shown me exactly who he was: an insecure little boy chasing validation wherever he could find it. He could've worked his way through the phone book, and it still wouldn't have filled the giant hole in his self-worth.

As Oprah so wisely said, "True forgiveness is when you can say, 'Thank you for that experience.'" So, thank you, Paul #3, for the experience of not being able to keep your dick in your pants. And with that, I'll be moving on to someone who can.

Forgive Yourself

Forgive yourself for accepting less than what you deserved. Forgive yourself for what you did when you were in survival mode. Give yourself grace.

Just as I know the sun will come out tomorrow, I know you will not only wrong another person in your lifetime, but you will be wronged as well. But you know what they say about anger: holding on to it is like drinking poison and expecting the other person to die. When you cling to your hurt, you cement yourself in the past and miss all the glory of the present.

Now, I'm not saying you should ignore your feelings in favor of an epic sunset, but there's a difference between acknowledging your pain and letting your mind splash around aimlessly in your anger like a kid at a waterpark.

When you forgive, you clear out the clutter and make space for the good stuff—joy, peace, maybe even some unexpected magic. Forgiveness means you're no longer giving others access to the sacred space of your thoughts. It's not about letting them off the hook—it's about letting *yourself* off the hook.

Think of it as cleaning out that mental junk drawer stuffed with resentment, overthinking, and maybe a stale granola bar. Hit the "refresh" button on your brain so you can finally welcome everything you actually want. And, as they say: to err is human, and to forgive is divine.

Turn the Mirror Back on You

Giving yourself grace is like untangling Christmas lights—it's hard, requires a lot of patience, and you don't really know if it's going to work. Whether you need to show compassion to yourself or others, here are some things that can help.

1. The first step is to accept what happened. Accept your feelings. Be sad, angry, hurt. Those are all valid emotions that need to be felt. Brushing your emotions under the rug will only come back to haunt you.
2. Forgiveness isn't like instant ramen; it takes time. Give yourself a couple of weeks to sit in your feelings and sort things out. Decide if the relationship is worth saving. Don't stick around in a situation that feels like wearing wet socks, no matter how sorry he/she may seem. If you do stay, lay down the law. Make it clear what won't fly moving forward. But give time, time.
3. Holding onto anger like it's your favorite handbag? Time to ask yourself *why?* Does it make you feel in control? Are you worried they'll hurt you again? Do you think forgiving means letting them off easy? Newsflash: You can't control their actions, but you can control your peace of mind. Stop replaying that tired old drama. Choose to move on or move forward—either way, you're the one who wins.

Heartbreak Kid

"'Tis better to have loved and lost than never to have loved at all."

—ALFRED, LORD TENNYSON

"Fuck you, Alfred. No! No, it's not. Right now, I wish I had never even laid eyes on his dumb ass." I have said this more times than I can count, starting back at my first boyfriend in kindergarten who didn't even know he was my boyfriend. Ugh! Men!

Sadly, peanut, heartbreak is part of the packaged deal here on earth. Big, crazy, deep heartbreak that can sneak up on us when we least expect it.

We think we can stumble through it with grace, but it's messy. We think we can make it hurt less, but we can't. How to make our head unhurt and our hearts unbreak is the $60-million question that has no quick answer. Jumping to cheery thoughts, like *I learned so much; the relationship served its purpose; I'm grateful he showed me who he was*, is all just a bunch of hooey when your heart's freshly gutted open.

Whether your BFF of the last fifteen years broke up with you or your "forever and more" turned out to be for a limited time only, the only way to put the pieces back together is to dive into the heartache any which way you choose. For me, healing every love lost looked different each time. But the one truth that remained was this: *The only way out is in.*

Pull up a seat, sister. It's time to get real.

Karaoke Blues

When I was in my twenties, I dated a guy who cheated on me like it was his personal Olympic event, and he was going for the gold. Each time it happened, I would break up with him in a storm of tears, screaming, "You're not even worth the mascara I'm ruining!" I would obsessively read through all of our text messages, dissecting every emoji and comma and looking for signs—signs that pointed to the inevitable and signs that he would never love anyone as much as he loved me.

But then came the last time. My heart, duct-taped together so many times in the past, barely held its shape. My spirit felt bruised and sucker-punched by each time he'd said, "I'll never do it again," only to turn around and do exactly that. Like the last sad puff of a candle before it goes out, I left. There was nothing left of me to burn.

Nights blurred into each other as I lay there, wrapped in his old sweatshirt, inhaling the faint smell of his Paco Rabanne cologne, hoping it would somehow imprint itself in my mind forever. I wanted to preserve his scent like a memory that might make up for all the broken ones.

The funny thing about heartbreak is that it doesn't always heal the way you expect it to. Sometimes, the best medicine isn't deep talks or dramatic gestures. Sometimes, healing is found not at the bottom of a pint of ice cream, a bottle of tequila, or in the arms of a new rebound but at Karaoke Bleu in Santa Monica, a hole-in-the-wall karaoke joint where parties of ten would come in with their bottles of alcohol in hand, ready to sing 4 Non Blondes and Billy Idol. And I would come in as a party of one, cradling my box of tissues like a blankie.

Yep, I sang my way through the healing process—one off-key ballad at a time. Mariah Carey's "I Don't Wanna Cry" was a favorite I belted out on repeat. Badly. Thank God those rooms were soundproof. It was my version of a one-woman concert, and let's just say Mariah had nothing to worry about from me.

Mimi Healed My Heart

After a few months of being known around Karaoke Bleu as "Crying Girl in Room Five," the relentless ache and emptiness in my chest was starting to morph. I was no longer scrolling through my text messages. I was no longer doing drive-bys each night to see whose car was in his driveway. I was starting to feel like I had a handle on love's broken echo.

Singing had unlocked something I didn't know I needed, a way to connect with my feelings that went deeper than ice cream or tequila ever could. Eyes closed, hand to heart, singing to my own pain like the Grammy committee was watching. I was hitting imaginary high notes while my heartbreak took a bow, and little by little, I began to mend.

Mimi got me. It was downright cathartic to scream from the depths of my soul, my voice cracking in all the right places. For months, all I could see was how broken I felt, but with Mariah on my side, each song was stitching my heart back together, one shaky verse at a time.

So, if you got fucked by love, grab a microphone or a hairbrush and try it. Kelly Clarkson's "Catch My Breath," Gabby Barrett's "I Hope," and Imogen Heap's "Hide and Seek" are all great places to start if you want to be depressed and fist-pump at the same time. It's scientifically proven that breakup songs can release dopamine and oxytocin, reducing stress and anxiety, like a form of music therapy. Let yourself feel what your heart is mourning. You can't heal what you won't look at, and sometimes, the only way through is with a bit of volume.

But don't forget to cancel his Netflix subscription from your account first. You're not going to finance his post-breakup binge. Reclaim your digital territory, stat.

Eating Ben & Jerry's, Praying to God, and Loving the Shit Out of My Pain

Though all of this is written about in greater detail in the Divorce chapter, of all my breakups, my divorce was the one that gave me my PhD in pain. Though it truly was best for everyone involved, seeing his wet signature on the final divorce paper was like having a piano dropped on my heart. My life looked like a shattered mosaic, pieces scattered across the floor, and I had no clue where to start picking them up.

Do I cry in front of the kids? What do I do with the coffee mugs we bought on vacation? How the fuck do I even begin to mend?

Every hour looked different. One minute, I'd feel like a fit, flirty queen. The next, I was fully cocooned in a blanket burrito, swearing I'd never leave the house again. The only warmth I felt was from my morning coffee—before the tequila made its grand entrance. And let's not forget: This was all during COVID. My rebound options were basically limited to masked grocery store flirting. "Ooh, nice cantaloupe," I'd say, hoping for a glimpse of someone's nose. That went nowhere.

So, I turned inward. Ice cream. Journaling. Rom-coms. Myself. I rediscovered all the little things I'd set aside during my marriage. As any married woman knows, there's this unspoken pressure to always look good for your spouse, to never *fully* control the remote, and to always, always put yourself last. But now? I was alone, haunted by memories of the "good ol' days," and in the midst of it all, I welcomed back some long-lost loves: dessert, Julia Roberts, and most importantly, me.

For seven months straight, I watched *Eat, Pray, Love* like it was my religion. Julia Roberts rebuilding her life after divorcing Billy Crudup was basically my emotional support animal. Her "ruin is the road to transformation" monologue? Yes, Julia. YES. You see me.

"Maybe my life hasn't been so chaotic. It's just the world that is, and the real trap is getting attached to any of it. Ruin is a gift. Ruin is the road to transformation."

Those words slapped me awake faster than my morning espresso. I didn't need some warm body next to me, snoring and drooling on my pillow. My bed was no longer a giant neon sign flashing, "VACANCY—ANYONE WITH A PULSE WELCOME." Because, I was transforming—and that was way better company than whatever I could drag home from the produce aisle.

A mountain of gooey, cheesy comfort food also became necessary. And science can back me up here. When you eat carbs, your brain throws a little party, releasing serotonin and dopamine—those feel-good chemicals that remind you your life isn't a complete dumpster fire. Sure, the happiness doesn't last forever (neither does queso), but it's enough to lift your mood and whisper, "Hey, you're still standing."

So eat up, buttercup! Because sometimes, the best way to fix a broken heart is with a dish full of mac 'n' cheese. Soul food isn't just for your stomach—it's for your sanity. And let me tell you, nothing says "you'll get through this" quite like biscuits smothered in gravy.

Listen, homie, I get it—nobody wants to sit with their hurt, but you can't just sweep it under the rug and hope it won't trip you up later. Pain doesn't come with an expiration date, so ignoring it is like leaving milk in the fridge—you're only setting yourself up for a stinky surprise later.

There's no "one-size-fits-all" for healing, so don't let anyone tell you how to mend your heart. Losing someone might feel like the end, but it's life clearing the brush, so you can find the right path forward. So, take a deep breath and let your heartache sit beside you for awhile—it's not here to break you; it's here to build you.

Turn the Mirror Back on You

Of all the organs in the body, the heart is the one that breaks over and over again, only to put itself back together, stronger than before. The pain won't consume you. It'll transform you. If you're feeling the sting of heartbreak, here are a few things to ponder between sad songs and double scoops of ice cream.

1. Are you really heartbroken, or are you just attached to someone who knew your coffee order? This is an important distinction to make, and one that can save

you hours of tears. You'll only learn the answer by getting quiet and investigating your pain.

2. What parts of yourself did you put on hold for this relationship? Dig out those "old friends" you haven't seen in a while and get to know yourself again! You now have more time for the one person you need the most: you. Pamper yourself today like the VIP you are.
3. Did you maybe, just maybe, ignore a few red flags? Like when they "forgot" your birthday or were weirdly protective of their phone? We've all been there, but every relationship is basically a crash course in learning what you don't want. So don't walk away without snagging those life lessons. Next time someone "just doesn't do labels," you'll know to hit the gas and swerve.

Help Me Help You Help Me

"Asking for help isn't giving up. It's refusing to give up."

—CHARLIE MACKESY, BADASS PHILOSOPHER AND MUSER OF LIFE

6:00 a.m.: What the fuck?! Is that a fog horn? No, it's your alarm bitching at you to get out of bed. Breakfast chaos ensues. Feed the kids, dogs, and spouse. Do you get fed? Not a chance.

8:30 a.m.: Drop the kids off at school. Drive feverishly down the 405 into the office to make it to your 9:00 a.m. meeting.

12:00 p.m.: Eat your boss's shitty birthday cake while he recounts boring highlights from his pickleball tournament.

> 1:00 p.m.: A phone call from school says one of your kids forgot their lunch. Accept defeat. Drive back to the school with a stale sandwich from the deli.
>
> 4:00 p.m.: Rush to the grocery store after work to collect the ingredients for dinner.
>
> 5:30 p.m.: Make dinner while having deep discussions about who's the strongest Avenger and "How much does the earth cost?"
>
> 8:00 p.m.: Do the homework hustle, followed by the bedtime struggle, which includes lots of "I'm not tired" and multiple glasses of water.
>
> 9:30 p.m.: Time to "clean up, clean up, everybody help." Except...everyone's asleep. But you.

As we saw in Boundaries Bitch, it's a universal truth that all women think they must carry the weight of the world (and the laundry basket) on their shoulders. It's not our fault! Society practically gift-wraps this nonsense and hands it to us. There are Pinterest boards dedicated to women who run marathons, lead board meetings, and breastfeed simultaneously. Cue the world's biggest eye roll.

So naturally, we go from being the CEO at work to the CEO at home. Delegation? Never heard of her. And what do we get for all this hustle? Surely there's a gold medal waiting somewhere, right? Spoiler alert: There's not. Maybe a half-hearted "good job" if you're lucky.

You're human. I repeat: You're *human*. Admitting you need help is not a sign of weakness. Yes, yes, I know we can do it all, but do we want to? No! Fuck that with a bag of hammers! Whether we're in need of an extra hand physically or spiritually, help is out there. *Just ask.*

Pass It On or Pass Out

Just because you can do forty-seven things a day doesn't mean you should. Asking for help isn't admitting defeat—it's acknowledging that even Wonder Woman has a support team. Whether it's passing off the grocery list, handing over the laundry, or delegating bath time, you're not waving a white flag. You're saying, "I'm the glue that holds this operation together, and in order to keep being amazing, I need some help."

The people in your life already know you're a superhero. You don't need to lasso every chore in sight to prove it. Besides, people secretly love feeling useful—so let your ten-year-old load the dishwasher, hand your spouse the to-do list, or ask your neighbor to grab the package off your porch. They'll feel like heroes and you might even get five minutes to drink your coffee while it's hot.

Help as a Prayer

Sometimes, no matter how hard you try to human, you just can't see the forest for the trees. We make plans and backup plans, run 'em by everyone with an opinion, then throw in another "just in case" plan, so we can guarantee ourselves as much control as possible.

That's the exact moment when you need to throw your hands up (jazz hands if you're really in trouble) and ask the Big Guy Upstairs for a little help. Don't believe in Him? No problem. Totally fine. Shout it into the universe, the void, or your mailbox even. The point isn't *where* you send the SOS—it's realizing that you're not the CEO of Holding It All Together, and something bigger than you is listening.

When life gets lifey, sometimes the best thing you can do is loosen your white-knuckle grip and say one word: "Help." You don't need some big, elaborate prayer—just you, messy, and hollering "Help!" into the sky like your grandmother was locked out of church. No fancy words. Just honesty. In *Plan B: Further Thoughts on Faith*, Anne Lamott——wrote, "The first great prayer is Help.... Help is a prayer that is always answered. It doesn't have to be the right words. It's the heart's cry for assistance..."

Something hears you. It always does. Asking for help is your way of saying, "I've done all I can do. Your turn, universe."

And somehow? The universe always gets the memo. Maybe it's a heart-to-heart with a friend who says the exact thing you needed to hear. Maybe it's a random conversation with a stranger that turns into an instant connection. Or maybe it's one door slamming so loud it shakes something loose in you—just in time for another to swing wide open. Whatever form it takes, it's like Postmates delivering cosmic blessings right on time.

But you have to *ask first.* I know you'd rather eat gas station sushi than admit you need help, but it's time to drop the act and admit you're human. It's admitting that maybe, just maybe, you need a hand, even if it's an invisible one. And that, my friend, is where the magic starts.

Turn the Mirror Back on You

If you're having trouble uttering the "H" word, ponder the following:

1. Are you constantly chasing the clock? If your day leaves you running on empty, speak up and ask someone who's not as busy as you to help lighten the load. Even if it's a friend's friend, help is available to you if you look. Most folks get a little boost from pitching in. Think of it this way: you're giving them a golden opportunity to be the hero for once.
2. What is it that you have to get done today? Be real here. Not everything on your to-do list needs to get done by the time your head hits the pillow. Make a list and only prioritize the things that are a priority—and don't even look at the things that are not.
3. Do you ever expect people to just magically know what you need? Like, you're struggling with three grocery bags and say something like, "Wow, I didn't realize avocados were so heavy!" Meanwhile, your friend is just standing there, completely oblivious. People can't read minds (tragic, I know). Instead of dropping hints that go nowhere, just say, "Hey, can you grab a bag?" Clear, direct, and way less frustrating.

I Don't Know

"There are years that ask questions, and moments that answer them."

—YOURS TRULY

Should you stay or should you go? Ask for the raise or keep letting them pay you in Monopoly money? Feel like life just dumped a big, heavy "figure it out" on your plate? Yeah, I get it. Sometimes every option feels about as appealing as ass cancer.

But guess what, sis? You're exactly where you're supposed to be. Not everyone has the courage to pause and ask, "Is this it, or could there be something better?" As we say in Texas, "You've got more guts than you can hang on a fence."

And speaking of guts, let's talk about yours—because learning to trust it is the ultimate cheat code in life. Your emotions? They're not just drama queens; they're little nudges trying to get your attention. They're clues, breadcrumbs leading you to your next move.

Emotions Are Your Friends

How many times have you stared in the mirror with tears streaming down your face as you repeated, "No, I'm OK. Really. Really, I am. I'm OK. I'm great. I feel fine. Waaaaaaaaaah!"

You are not Annette Bening in *American Beauty.* Stop with the performance. The Oscar's not happening. You're not OK—*and that's OK.*

We freak out over our emotions because they've been vilified in our culture. If we're sad, we try not to be sad. If we're angry, we try not to be angry. As one of my first acting coaches taught me, "The only way out is in." You can't fix something you're not willing to look at, so dive into your feelings. They're just little alerts from your body saying, "Head's up, here's what's happening today."

Take anxiety, for example. Maybe your morning commute to the office has you feeling like a shaky Chihuahua on espresso—jittery, on edge, and one honk away from a full meltdown. Ask yourself: *Am I exhausted? Overworked? Giving 98 percent of my energy to everyone else and surviving on caffeine and sheer spite?* Or maybe—*gasp*—you're just tired of your boss treating you like office wallpaper during the weekly staff meeting.

Sure, one option is to stand up, flip the table, and dramatically declare, *"IT'S MY TURN TO SPEAK TED!"* But let's be honest—that's probably not the career move you're going for. First, you've gotta calm your tits long enough to figure out what's actually going on beneath the spiral. Name the feeling, give it some breathing room, and *then* have a level-headed conversation where you say something wildly revolutionary like, "Hey, I'd love to be heard. I have some ideas worth sharing."

Because here's the thing: You can't control your emotions, but you can control how you behave around them. Emotions are messengers, not dictators. So when in doubt, don't run from them—*get curious.*

Classic example of dodging your emotions? You're dating a guy who's cute, sweet, and emotionally available…to his fantasy football league. He knows how to pick a great sushi spot but somehow forgets how to pick up the phone when you're crying in your car at 7:00 p.m. on a Tuesday. To put it mildly, he makes mediocrity feel aspirational.

And then, like clockwork, that tiny voice in your head whispers, *"Maybe I'm overthinking it?"*

You're not overthinking. You're under-listening—to your gut, your intuition, your internal Beyoncé screaming, "We don't do crumbs anymore, baby."

You're caught in the classic "but he's not *that* bad" trap. Spoiler: Not being "that bad" isn't the same as being good. If you're feeling consistently confused, overlooked, or like you need to mentally build a case just to justify staying, there's your answer.

Doubt doesn't just show up to kill the vibe. It's your inner wisdom flicking the lights on and whispering, "Let's take a closer look, shall we? You're worth more than this."

Don't Doubt Your Doubt

Doubt hits when your old beliefs are squaring up with your new ones—a full-on internal title fight. Past You is in one corner, throwing familiar jabs, clinging to comfort. Future You's in the other, coming in hot with fresh energy and bold moves. It's messy, it's uncomfortable—and it's exactly what growth looks like. Feeling unsure just means you're in the ring, fighting for what's best for *you.*

Let's face it: Needs change, values shift, and the only thing guaranteed in life is change. You're not supposed to be the same person you were five, ten, or fifteen years ago! We're here to grow, and growth isn't some cute, straight path—it's more like a roller coaster designed by a drunk engineer: loops, dips, and those "hold on for dear life" moments that make you question everything.

But here's the trick: Don't get stuck obsessing over the dark tunnels or that nerve-wracking climb to the top. Stop worrying about what you can't see coming—it's exhausting and steals your joy. Now, brace yourself because I'm about to flip your perspective: The reason you don't know what to do right now is *because you're not meant to!*

Yep, read that again. You're in the in-between—that awkward, soul-stretching middle ground that feels less like a spiritual journey and more like puberty for your personality. You're not who you used to be, but you're not quite whoever the hell you're becoming either. That confusion you're feeling? That restless, itchy, *existential shrug* that makes you want to change your life, your hair, and your Wi-Fi provider? That's not failure. That's transition, homie.

Sometimes clarity doesn't come on your timeline, and that's OK. If there's one thing I've learned, it's that answers show up when you're ready—not when you're in overthinking mode. Trust the process, even when it feels messy. You're exactly where you need to be. Breathe, and know the answers will find you.

Divine Timing Is Always on Time

You might be in the dark right now, saying, "Fuck if I know what to do!" Give yourself grace. Trust the timing of your life. *Trust the timing of your life.*

I knew I was going to get a divorce years before I actually got one. And all those hours I spent tormenting myself with, "Is this the moment I leave, or should I wait till tomorrow after dinner?" never made the actual day come any faster.

We waste so much energy freaking out in limbo that we miss the good stuff happening right in front of us. When I have no fucking clue what to do, I focus on what I do know.

You know you love hanging with your kids? Take them to the park. You know you're a boss at work? Show up early and stay late. Love cooking? Whip up that fancy recipe you've been eyeing.

You don't need a life plan—just do the next small thing that makes you happy. Sip your coffee outside, get your nails done, or wander a new grocery store (weirdly therapeutic).

Nobody's grading you on how fast you figure it out. Whether the light bulb clicks today or in ten years, you'll know when it's time. Until then, follow your happy as laid out in the previous chapter. It's the best GPS you've got.

Turn the Mirror Back on You

The average person makes thirty-five thousand decisions a day. It's natural to feel doubt over at least one of them! Here are some questions that will help you move forward.

1. Be brutally honest with yourself. What makes you happy? The answer might scare you. It might disappoint

others. But most of all, if you're struggling with indecision, consider whether this might be because you're trying to live someone else's life rather than your own.

2. When doubt sits on my shoulders like a whiny little bitch, and I can't get clear on a decision, I pretend it's my last day on earth. If you were to become God's roommate tomorrow, are you OK with this current situation? Are you going to stay at your ho-hum job because you don't want to disappoint your coworkers? Are you staying in your sucky marriage for the kids? What chances would you take if you knew you had nothing to lose? It's OK if you can't make the moves you want to make *today*, but getting clarity is the first step to set those wheels in motion.
3. What are your core values? Is your current state betraying the principles that you value in life (for example, honesty, family, respect, and communication)? If you can get clear on what your core values are and make them non-negotiable, chances are you'll get unstuck.
4. Journal like a motherfucker! The church of journaling is where I worship—and when life gets lifey, this is the kind of religion that you want on your side. I'll get into it more in the actual Journaling chapter, but this can be the quiet haven where you get super acquainted with you: Your wants, needs, desires, dreams, likes, dislikes, disappointments, and hopes all come out on the page. It's your very own verbal vomit that'll give you even the slightest hint of clarity in times of uncertainty.

Intuition

"The force will be with you, always."

—OBI-WAN KENOBI, WISE JEDI MASTER, AND WEARER OF INCREDIBLY FASHION-FORWARD ROBES

Hindsight's a bitch, isn't it? How many times have you thought, "Shit. I knew I should've listened to my gut!"—only to ignore it again when your single, forty-four-year-old friend who still says things like "That's my jam" gives you life advice over bottomless mimosas.

Humans are the only species with instinct…that they actively ignore. Every animal listens to its gut—except us. Can you imagine if Sally the salmon was like, "Nah, I'm swimming downstream this year." She'd miss spawning season and die confused in a koi pond.

You know what's up. *You* know the relationship's trash. *You* know your boss is a jerk. *You* know your kid's new friend has future arsonist energy. *You* know not to lease that apartment with cracked walls, haunted vibes, and a highway view. Stop talking yourself out of what's painfully obvious—your gut's smarter than you think.

Intuition vs. Fear

"But Sarah, how do I know if it's my intuition or fear?"

Ah, the age-old question! Dear reader, perk up: Intuition is like that friend who's brutally honest but always spot-on. It hits you with a sucker punch to the gut—straight, no chaser—before your brain can start spinning stories. You might not like what it's saying, but deep down, you know it's right. There's no debate, no overanalyzing, and it tells *one* story. If it walks like a duck and quacks like a duck…it's not a beaver in a duck suit. It's a damn duck.

Think of it as your higher self sliding into your DMs with cosmic clarity. Even when the truth sucks, intuition leaves you feeling clearer than before. It's like turning on the high beams in the middle of a dark road—suddenly, you can see exactly where you're headed. You may not love what you see, but at least you're not driving blind anymore. That kind of clarity is priceless. It cuts through the noise, the second-guessing, the people-pleasing fog. And when we start taking our IRL cues from that place, everything changes for the better.

Fear, however, is a funny little fucker. It's like a loud, paranoid roommate who constantly assumes the worst. It's messy, dramatic, and can't stop spinning what -if scenarios like it's training for a conspiracy theory podcast. It makes you question everything as it's the ultimate drama queen. Whereas your intuition tells you *one* story, fear tells you a *million.* "What if he didn't call me back because he's cheating on me? Or dead? Or he was an eye witness to international embezzlement and is now in witness protection?" You can talk yourself in or out of any story because you are not rooted in any kind of critical thinking.

The reason? Thank your amygdala! It's the tiny drama queen in your brain whose full-time job is to freak out. She's basically the smoke detector of your nervous system: loud, panicky, and reacts to burnt toast like it's a five-alarm fire. Great when you're being chased by Pennywise—less helpful when you're overthinking a two-word text. God forbid you receive a thumbs-up when you wanted a kissing emoji—you might as well start digging your grave.

The cold, hard truth is: your brain isn't wired for happiness—it's wired for survival. To that fear-driven part of you, *predictable misery feels safer than unpredictable possibility.* It would rather keep you stuck in a familiar hell than risk an unfamiliar heaven—because "change" is its least favorite word. But hey, no one ever soared by clinging to the ledge—so take the damn leap. Even if the future feels uncertain, even if heaven looks unfamiliar—jump anyway. That's where the good stuff lives.

As Cheryl Strayed said, "Fear, to a great extent, is born of a story we tell ourselves." You may not be able to turn off your fear completely, but you can certainly choose to tell yourself a different story. Your biggest nemesis is your uncontrolled mind. So, slap it around a few times and make it your bitch. *You* are in charge.

Don't Decorate Shit with Flowers

A few years ago, my agents pitched me a job I wouldn't touch with a ten-foot pole. The script was an absolute disaster. Trying to make it work would have been like trying to nail Jell-O to a wall. The plot holes were massive and the dialogue felt like it was written by someone who's heard English in passing. I told them repeatedly I wasn't interested. But they kept polishing that turd like it was the Hope Diamond, throwing money figures around like confetti, and eventually…I caved. Not because I believed in it, but because I didn't want to let anyone down.

Cut to day one: The director didn't know what story he was telling: A Magic 8 Ball had more clarity. The writer wrote scenes mid-shoot like we were workshopping a high school play, and I'm pretty sure the sound guy still thinks the blinking red light means "go get coffee." It was a circus where nobody brought the tent—and I knew it from the jump. My gut had practically sent me a singing telegram that said "RUN." But I didn't listen.

I ignored the red flags, duct-taped my instincts, and went anyway. Why? Pressure. Because of the illusion that saying "yes" makes you a good person, a team player. It was the noble, collaborative thing to do, right? It proved that I was willing to roll up my sleeves and help salvage the sinking ship. I thought, "Maybe it'll turn around."

It did not.

Here's what I learned: No amount of perfume can cover the stench of something that feels off. You can throw money at it, dress it up, light it well—but if it's wrong, it's wrong. And when your intuition is yelling "Absolutely not," it's not being dramatic. It's being *protective*. It's trying to keep you from trading your time, energy, and sanity for something that was already dead on arrival.

So stick to your guns, youngblood. Learn to disappoint people before you disappoint *yourself*. Your intuition doesn't come with fireworks and neon signs. It comes quietly. It taps you on the shoulder and says, *This isn't it.* And when you ignore it long enough, the fallout isn't just a bad experience—it's a little bruise on your self-trust.

You can dress up a bad decision with logic, money, or ego—but you can't un-feel the knowing. The truth was always there. I just didn't want to listen.

It may feel hard at first, but the more you listen to your gut, the less you'll end up apologizing to yourself in hindsight. And trust me: Your "no" is not a missed opportunity—it's a power move.

Turn the Mirror Back on You

You may not like what your intuition is telling you, but be as brave as the person who invented the vibrator and tune in to it.

1. Sit your cute self down, close your eyes, and ask your question. Five minutes of stillness can be life-changing. You'll feel a gentle nudge in the right direction. Your gut's got a strong signal. You just have to shut out the noise long enough to hear it.
2. If you need another reminder, fear shows up like an uninvited ex—tight chest, racing thoughts, full-body chaos. Intuition though? It whispers from the gut, quiet but steady. And cool fact: Your gut literally has neurons. That's why it's deemed your second brain. So if something feels off, believe it—your stomach's smarter than half your group chat.
3. When life is fucking us sideways, Mother Nature's remarkable healing touch can do wonders. It can help you decompress and think more clearly. Don't be afraid to go out and hug some trees or talk to a squirrel. You'll be surprised by what you get back.

4. Sometimes, listening to yourself is about knowing when a thought needs to leave your head and enter the conversation. Give it two days—if it's still tap-dancing through your brain, you need to voice it. Even if the other person doesn't want to hear it. It's not about them—it's about *you* and what *you need.*

Journaling

"Listen you piece of fuck, go shit yourself."

—MY JOURNAL ENTRY FROM MAY 14, 2001

William Wordsworth said it a little differently: "Fill your paper with the breathings of your heart." Honestly, I'm not sure what his journaling game looked like, but I like to think even Wordsworth had a messy notebook somewhere, scribbled with, "Fanny looked at me weird today. What's her deal?"

Of all the self-care strategies I've tried (and I've tried *everything* short of goat yoga), the most consistent and rewarding has been journaling. It's like a mental detox, a free therapy session, and a personal roast battle rolled into one.

Journaling isn't some newfangled mindfulness trend—Marcus Aurelius was scribbling his feelings way back in the second century AD. Imagine this powerful Roman emperor hunched over his scroll, lamenting over Cleopatra: "Cleo, why dost thou ghost me? Oh! Built you a whole city during lunch today. Had a dream I died of something called pneumonia. Hmm…" Even rulers needed a place to dump their emotional clutter.

When you take pen to paper, you're gifted a conversation with the smartest, wisest person in the room: your deepest self. You get a front-row seat to your emotional operating system. Not to mention, on paper, anything goes! You can have comments that are all coat and no knickers, be superficial as shit, write that you're gonna shit in your ex-husband's girlfriend's face all because she took your daughter to ice cream—and no one will judge you for it! It's the greatest pressure-releasing valve there is, all courtesy of a judgment-free zone.

When I get into a conflict that turns my insides out, the first thing I do is grab pen and paper and let all my thoughts swim in a stream of consciousness. Usually, I begin with, "If only they would just listen!" And then, I list what idiots they are and everything they did wrong; eventually, after a few "What the fuck do they know anyways?" I find my way to my own emotions. To the hurt and the pain that are lying in the center of my heart.

Remember our little friend, the amygdala, from the Intuition chapter? (Yes, that almond-shaped troublemaker in your brain.) Well, it's back for a sequel. When we're stressed or upset, it hijacks our emotions, flipping us into fight-or-flight mode. Journaling is like handing it a juice box and telling it to take a seat. Writing soothes the amygdala, calming the chaos and letting your logical brain step in. That's when you start connecting dots, finding insight—not just into our own perspective but theirs, too. This is the fast train to feeling better.

After one of my many fights with one of my boyfriends, this was my entry: "You're so fucking dumb, you couldn't find a tit in a strip club—go shit yourself." (I thought I was very clever throwing him an alternative to "go fuck yourself," even if it was just on paper.) Was it cathartic? Yes. Did I feel like a Shakespearean insult genius? Also yes. Did I ever say it to him? Not in those words. But after a good journaling session, I uncovered the real issue: *I felt insecure when you stayed out till 4:00 a.m. and ignored my texts.* I was able to find the center of my pain and then communicate it in such a way that we could both hear each other out. That kind of communication is a lot more effective than, "Sure, it's a cock, but smaller. Eat rocks."

That's the magic of journaling—it helps you find the truth beneath the chaos, so you can actually communicate like a grown-up instead of lobbing insults like a middle schooler with a thesaurus.

And this OG method of mental detox is free! So grab a notebook, rage-write like you're penning the angriest YA novel ever, and say things you wouldn't say out loud, like, "Megan was always a shit friend with beady little eyes. She looks like a rat. You can't trust people who look like rodents." It soothes the mental gremlin, calming your nervous system, so you can think clearly. It's like pressing "defrost" on a frozen windshield—you start seeing what's really there.

Turn the Mirror Back on You

Even if you've never been the "Dear Diary" type, it's never too late to start spilling your guts. Here's how to dive in without overthinking it.

1. Make it stupid easy for yourself. Keep a pen and notebook by your nightstand or use your phone. I'd be mortified if anyone saw my Notes app. Your deepest

wisdom is found within. You just need to make the space and start scribbling.

2. Don't know where to start? Find a quiet spot and let your brain spill. No filter, no rules. Who cares if you go from "I hope you step on a Lego" to "Pepperoni really elevates an Italian sub"? This isn't a Pulitzer Prize submission—it's your space. Messy is encouraged. Doodle if words won't come. Feeling bold? Make a vision board full of wild dreams you've never said out loud.
3. At first, journaling might feel like a chore, but trust me, repetition is magic. Do it daily, even if it's just three sentences or a random thought. Before you know it, it'll feel like a regular date with your BFF—except this bestie is always available, nonjudgmental, and really, really good at keeping secrets.

Judge Not Lest Ye Be Judged

"We can never judge the lives of others, because each person knows only their own pain and renunciation. It's one thing to feel that you are on the right path, but it's another to think that yours is the only path."

—PAULO COELHO, FROM THE ALCHEMIST

Girl! You know you do it! You've been judging other women since low-rise jeans and Von Dutch hats were trending! You see a girl walk by and immediately think, "Oh wow, bold choice on that outfit…must be laundry day." From who she's sleeping with, to her Instagram captions, to her cosmetic procedures, to how she raises her kids or spends her money—you've got opinions, and you serve them like hors d'oeuvres at a *Real Housewives* reunion.

But rest assured, buttercup, it's not just you. It's *all* of us. Judging is practically a team sport—equal parts insecurity, boredom, and projection wrapped in a tight little smirk. It's a human pastime we all engage in. It happens faster than a sneeze, and the next thing you know, you're saying things like, "Melissa cheated on David. She's such a slut. You could tell by those tight yoga pants she wears that crease right at her hoo-ha. It's basically a neon sign pointing to her vagina."

Karma has a wicked sense of humor, so unless you reincarnated in this lifetime as a saint, you may want to keep those judgments to yourself, or the joke may be on you.

When the Tables Turned

I became the punchline in my twenties. Remember my very chaste, Middle Eastern, Southern upbringing? I scowled and scoffed and turned my nose up at any ho-bag who cheated. Until…I became the ho-bag.

Cheating on my college boyfriend with my singing paramour became the juiciest scandal on campus when I was at Southern Methodist University. It was like *Gossip Girl*: Texas Edition. My best friend, Julie, dumped me, claiming I'd be coming for her boyfriend next; my lunch table exiled me faster than a reality show contestant, and the rumors were relentless: "Once a cheater, always a cheater." Not one person asked, "Why did you do it?"

Now, I'm not advocating cheating, but let me paint the picture—my relationship was on life support. We were basically glorified roommates who occasionally argued about the thermostat and gave each other high-fives out of obligation. Oh, and his dad? Full-on hitting on me, saying, "We could make beautiful music together." (Yes, you read that right. So many ewws. Also get a better line, old man.) We were already done, but the campus jury had decided I was "Lowlife Barnacle of the Year." The judgment stung, sure, but here's the thing: No one gave a damn about the context. People weren't interested in what led up to it, how lonely or stuck I felt, or whether the relationship had already quietly flatlined. They wanted a villain. And I made a convenient one.

Because let's be real—judging someone is easier than empathizing with them. It takes zero effort to gossip. It takes emotional maturity to ask, "What happened?" or better yet, "Are you okay?"

Life has a funny way of evening the score. And as I laid out in the Grace over Grudges chapter, karma's got excellent aim.

These days, when I hear about someone cheating, I don't clutch my pearls or grab a gavel. People are messy. Relationships are *messier.* It's rarely as black and white as the cafeteria scandal machine makes it out to be. As the brilliant Esther Perel said, "Affairs are not always about finding someone new—they're about seeking something that's missing...emotionally, mentally, or physically." And you know what? That's not something you learn sitting at a lunch table with a side of judgment and fries.

Life isn't a morality play; it's a masterclass in compassion. People aren't villains—they're human. And sometimes, understanding that is the only way we grow. Everyone is a hot mess at some point in their lives, and to believe you are better just because your rock bottom looks different from theirs makes you about as sharp as a marble. Unless you're the one who's behind those closed doors, you don't know what's going on. Don't judge. Everyone's doing the best they can in the moment they're in.

"Did You See What She Did?"

And just when you think you've figured out how to be a decent, evolved human—life hands you a kid! Nothing humbles you faster than parenting. Suddenly, all that hard-won wisdom flies out the window, and you're negotiating with a tiny, irrational dictator with a glitter addiction.

Parenting is like competing on *America's Got Talent*—except instead of dazzling the judges with your tap-dancing skills, you're juggling a screaming toddler, a boiling pot of pasta, and a meltdown about the wrong color cup, all while smiling like, "No big deal, I've got this!" Spoiler alert: You don't. Nobody does. We're all just hoping Simon Cowell doesn't show up to critique our bedtime routines.

And let me tell you, the shade you get as a parent is unmatched—more than from a skyscraper at sunset. *Two home births including a breech twin home birth? Co-sleeping? Breastfeeding past a year?* Oh, I checked every nerve on the "Parenting Choices That Make Suburban Moms Gasp" checklist. The commentary was endless: "You're still breastfeeding? He's one. Give it up already!" "Home birth? Were you auditioning for *Little House on the Prairie*?" "Co-sleeping? He'll never learn independence." Well, that same "clingy" baby is now sixteen, six feet tall, and wouldn't cuddle with me unless I Venmo'd him fifty bucks and promised not to tell my friends.

The level of judgment was Olympic-tier, and the unsolicited advice came faster than a toddler on a sugar high. Your judgement of someone doesn't define *them*—it defines *you* as a certified twat-bag. You don't know what someone's going through. Who are you to assume you're better only because you do things differently? Maybe the mom handing her kid an iPad at dinner worked an eighty-hour week and needs a break.

No one's perfect. Judging others just sets you up for a fall when your own flaws come to light (and trust me—they will). I'm an inglorious fucking bastard myself from time to time and have done things I sure as hell swore I'd never do, but unless you've sat in their silence, felt their panic at 2:00 a.m., and paid rent in their reality, you've got no business throwing stones.

We're all going to the same place in the end, so instead of putting all that energy into judging someone when you have no idea why they did what they did, how about you turn that effort around on yourself or even offer to be of service to the other person? Save the energy for something useful—or better yet, be kind.

And if you just can't help yourself?

Judge all you want—just keep the verdict to yourself.

Turn the Mirror Back on You

You're not Judge Judy. No one's paying you for your verdict, so try these on for size before you give someone your two cents.

1. There are three sides to every story: his, hers, and the truth. Do you know the full story? You may only be seeing one side. Be fair and don't make assumptions.
2. How would you feel if someone else judged you in this situation? Put yourself in their shoes. Would you want the same treatment, or would compassion sound a little better?
3. Is your judgment coming from a place of truth—or are your insecurities throwing a little temper tantrum? We've all taken cheap shots at others to feel better about ourselves—welcome to being human. But if judging

someone gives you that temporary "I'm superior" high, guess what—you're not. Maybe hit the brakes and check yourself. Deal with your stuff before coming for someone else's.

Karma

"Karma isn't a bitch—it's a mirror."

—UNKNOWN, STEALTHY LITTLE MINX

What goes around comes around. What you sow is what you reap. He who digs pits for others will fall in them himself. In other words? Karma's a bitch of a waitress that doesn't even have a menu—you get served what you deserve.

Call it whatever you want, but since most of us were munchkins on the playground, we had a knack for calling out injustice: bullies who used their fists instead of their words, BFFs who pinky-swore their loyalty but stole your candy when you weren't looking, and all the kids who cut you in line when it was pizza day in the cafeteria.

"That's not fair!" Cue the inner five-year-old stomping her foot and yelling at the drama. But here's where the metaphysics of karma swoop in to save the day. Karma is basically like a boomerang: Whatever energy is thrown out will come flying back. Call it the laws of physics or cosmic payback, but you get what you give. So, if someone wants to swipe your slice of pizza? Bingo! You don't need to steal theirs out of revenge because their karma is already in motion. That energy's gonna come back around and hit them...probably when they least expect it and most deserve it.

Your job isn't to settle the score—it's to stay in alignment. Keep your energy clean, your actions intentional, and your side of the street shiny. Because the last thing you want is the universe throwing shade in the form of your own bad vibes boomeranging back in heels.

You get what you put out.

Karma Is Also Your BFF

Karma is not all gloom and doom! It can also be your biggest fan rooting for you and waiting to bless you with all the good stuff when the time is right. But don't forget—those rewards aren't handed out for free. The universe keeps a secret scoreboard, and when you're out there spreading good vibes and being a top-tier human, karma's ready to show up and shower you with blessings. *You get what you put out.*

Picture this: You're in line at the grocery store, and the person ahead of you is having a total nightmare moment. Their card gets declined, and they're fumbling, red-faced, trying to figure it out. You step up, pay for their groceries, and walk away with a warm, fuzzy feeling, not expecting anything in return. You just did it because kindness matters, right? Fast-forward a few days, and bam—the universe hits you with some good karma. Maybe you get an unexpected promotion, or you find a hundred-dollar bill tucked into a jacket you haven't worn since last winter. That's karma coming back around, reminding you that even small acts of kindness can return tenfold. *You get what you put out.*

Good Vibes Only When Life Is Lifey

When life smacks you with some mind-blowing nonsense? Don't go pointing fingers at "bad karma," like the universe is some petty ex out to get you. It's here to help you grow even if that growth feels like getting pantsed in front of your crush. Every plot twist has a purpose—though sometimes it's hidden under a giant pile of *WTF.*

And while you're wading through those *WTF* moments, there's always something worth noticing. Gratitude isn't about perfection—it's about presence. It's about noticing the softness of your kid's hand in yours, or the way your dog looks at you like you hung the moon. It's the comfort of your favorite sweatshirt on a cold day, the way a good song feels like a lifeline, or the quiet satisfaction of a warm meal after a long week. Those are the gifts life hands you every day, even in the middle of chaos. It doesn't mean pretending things are OK when they're not; it means holding space for the mess and the magic at the same time.

When you lean into gratitude, it shifts everything. Not in an instant, not in some cheesy "manifest your dreams overnight" way. But slowly, steadily, like the tide rolling in. It opens your eyes to what's already good, so you can believe in what's still possible. Life isn't perfect, but it's still here. And so are you. So, take a breath. Look around. And let yourself notice the wonder woven through the mess. That's the kind of magic the universe was trying to show you all along.

Turn the Mirror Back on You

Karma's a bitch, but it can also be our best friend if we remember that life is on our side. Here are some ways to intentionally befriend karma instead of seeing it as the dark cloud hanging above you:

1. Focus on you, not the drama. Feeling jealous or craving revenge? Ask yourself why. "What is this trying to teach me?" Seriously, flip the script. The lesson might suck, but growth mode is activated. You're not here to be petty—you're here to level up. And nothing accelerates that glow-up faster than turning pain into power.
2. Don't be an asshole. Groundbreaking, right? But really—words and actions have receipts. Choose kindness. Pay it forward. Build up that good karma piggy bank because you will need it someday.
3. Skip the popcorn at your enemy's downfall. When you hear something bad happened to your high school nemesis, keep it clean. Can't send good vibes? Stay neutral and let the universe do its thing. Not your circus, not your monkeys.

Kids

"When your children are teenagers, it's important to have a dog so that someone in the house is happy to see you."

—NORA EPHRON, THE ROM-COM QUEEN AND MY FOREVER WRITING MUSE—NO ONE COULD MAKE HEARTBREAK AND ROAST CHICKEN HIT YOU RIGHT IN THE FEELS LIKE SHE COULD.

Giving birth is like shoving a watermelon through a straw, and then in a blink, you're handed a PhD in anxiety wrapped in a baby blanket. You worry twenty-four seven, cry over Goldfish crackers, and debate the ethics of screen time like you're on a parenting panel at Harvard—but somehow, one crooked smile or a sleepy "I love you" makes it all worth it. This is an ode to our chaotic, lovable ankle-biters—those tiny tyrants who hijack your snacks, stretch your patience, break your sleep, and make you question your sanity at least twice before noon.

At first, it's late-night breathing checks, tiny chests and tiny colds, princess Band-Aids, and magic kisses for every scrape. *The minutes feel like years*. Then, it's Minecraft, Roblox, and Skibidi Toilet (whatever that is). The princess dresses get donated, replaced by Forever 21 fits and daily debates about crop tops and two-pieces, and you find yourself quietly mourning the days she reached for your hand without thinking. One minute, you're their safe place—the go-to for carpool tea about who "snapped" who and the latest middle school drama. And then the next, they've passed driver's ed, and you're left marveling at how the school drop-offs you rushed through, became the memories you'd give anything to slow down.

The years feel like minutes.

There's a cruel observation floating around that states that 75 percent of all the time you will ever spend with your child is done by the time they're twelve. Like water between your fingers, the time simply slips away. Soak it up because no matter how old they are now, there'll never be this small again.

Go from What's Up to What's Really Up

I know you're tired. The work deadline is looming, and the laundry's multiplying. But no matter how chaotic life gets, be curious. Skip the usual "How was your day?" because let's be real: That question is like eating plain rice with a side of more plain rice. Instead, go deeper. Ask questions that make them think:

> "What made you happy today?"
>
> "What's something funny that happened at school?"

"Did you help anyone today?"

When you ask your kids specific questions that make them actually think, you get a front-row seat to who they are on a soul level. Don't let "Here's your chicken nuggets now do your homework" be the deepest convo you have all week.

Make Time for the Small Stuff, So They'll Tell You the Big Stuff

Look, I get it—you don't want to watch another YouTube video of MrBeast or some snotty twelve-year-old millionaire unboxing sneakers. But giving them five seconds of your attention shows you care about what they care about. Listen to the small stuff now, and they'll trust you with the big stuff later.

Once puberty hits, kids turn into cats: moody, aloof, and only coming around when they need food. But even through the eye rolls and silent treatments, love them harder than their moods. If you invest in their world before they shut their doors, they'll know they can come to you when life gets real.

And it will get real. One day, out of nowhere, you're explaining how babies actually get made, and why safe sex isn't just a suggestion. Next, you're having serious talks about drugs, praying your words don't come off as some out-of-touch lecture. These convos are tough—but being open and honest makes all the difference. Share your own mistakes (sparingly—no one wants a full TMI download from Mom) and show them you get it.

Most importantly, make space for their firsts: first crush, first heartbreak, first bra, first period. Holding your sobbing fourteen-year-old after some pubescent heartbreaker shatters their world might just wreck you too. So, keep a box of Kleenex handy—for both of you.

Turn the Mirror Back on You

I know you can't even take a piss in silence, but one day your tits will be down to your knees, and you'll have to bribe your kids to come visit you at Christmas. Shut your computer. Those emails can wait.

1. DIY trivia night: Instead of letting your older kids scroll TikTok all weekend, have them come up with family trivia questions and host a trivia night. You'll laugh, you'll cry—and learn way more than you bargained for. Bonus: Instant core memory unlocked.
2. Dinner takeover: Let the kids pick dinner a couple nights a week and help make it. They feel important; you get free kitchen labor—it's a win-win.
3. Parenting throwback check: Think to how you were parented. What worked? What made you want to blast emo music in your room? Take the good stuff (my mom rarely yelled) and toss the bad (she did rock the silent treatment—hard pass). Break the cycle. Be better.

Laughter

"Laughter is poison to fear."

—GEORGE R. R. MARTIN, THE AUTHOR WHO GAVE US RIDICULOUS EYE CANDY IN GAME OF THRONES

What's the alternative—cry? Frown? Collect extra wrinkles from a furrowed brow? Life loves throwing banana peels at your feet just when you think you've got it together. Sure, crying has its place (looking at you, *Titanic*, and *My Girl*—the scene with the bees? Get fucked), but when life gets lifey, you've got two options: drama or comedy.

Drama comes with puffy eyes, snotty noses, and a very uncute red face. Comedy? You laugh, lift your spirits, and give yourself a mini mental vacation. The problems are still there—but seeing them with a lighter heart might just change the whole game. It's your choice, champ.

I know you want to cry because the relationship didn't work out. But what if you laugh because he's such a moron instead?

Poor thing will spend the rest of his pathetic life chasing you down while you're on a yacht in Saint-Tropez with Lenny Kravitz feeding you grapes and licking tequila off your back. Your car broke down on the way to work? Split your sides at the fucking timing of it! Tell a few stupid jokes to the AAA driver who's on his way. You burned dinner for your entire family? Cackle as the fire alarm makes everyone a little deaf, and you decide to order pizza. Fewer dishes to clean up now!

Laughter Breeds Confidence

When you can laugh in the face of life's dumpster fires, you're not just cracking a joke—you're staging a full-blown coup against chaos. Problems *hate* being laughed at. It's like yanking off their villain cape, muting their dramatic theme song, and relegating them to the role of "awkward background extra" in your blockbuster life. The second you laugh, they lose their sting. It's like popping the balloon of doom: *Poof*—gone. And laughing isn't just a mood booster; it's a full-body power-up! It's like your soul's personal trainer, giving your nervous system a chill pill, your blood a pep talk, and your immune system a high-five. Or, as the legendary Bob Newhart put it, "Laughter gives us distance. It allows us to step back, deal with it, and move on." Translation? Laugh now, slay later. Life's messy—but you're funnier.

Picture this: Your kid dumps a sippy cup of milk into your purse, and your dog, clearly taking notes, decides your freshly shampooed carpet needs a "mud modern art" installation. What's your move? Cry? Spiral into a pit of despair? Sure, those are options—but let's be real, you've already aced the tear-streaked meltdown routine. Time to level up. Laugh.

Not a polite chuckle—go full-on cackle. Laugh until your abs hurt and your kid starts questioning your sanity. It might feel unhinged, but it's the *good* kind of unhinged—the kind that reminds everyone, including yourself, that you're the ringmaster of this glorious circus.

And the real plot twist: Every disaster is just a future story waiting for its spotlight. Your epic parenting fail? Tomorrow's punchline. That time you locked yourself out of the house in pajamas and bunny slippers? Instant crowd-pleaser. The car that broke down on the way to your dream job interview? That's not a tragedy—it's Netflix special material. Life's bloopers aren't here to ruin you; they're here to build your highlight reel. Why waste them crying when you could be hoarding comedy gold?

The trick is all in your perspective. Problems *want* to be taken seriously. They thrive on your frustration, your stress, your tears. But when you laugh, you shrink them down to bite-sized nuisances. Suddenly, they're not towering villains—they're tiny gremlins you can flick away like crumbs on a table. Laughter puts you back in the director's chair. You're holding the remote, flipping the script, and editing your worst days into the kind of dark comedy you'll still be cracking jokes about years from now.

And let's face it: Life is going to keep hurling curveballs. It's part of the deal. But when you've got a sense of humor, you're not just surviving—you're hitting grand slams. The next time the universe throws a pie in your face, don't let it win. Wipe it off, lick your fingers, and laugh. Remember, disasters are temporary, but your ability to find the joke? That's forever.

So go ahead—laugh loud, laugh boldly, and remind the world that you're unstoppable. Life may be messy, but your humor and resilience? Those are your superpowers. Disasters are temporary, but your confidence? That's permanent. Your ability to laugh in the chaos doesn't just make you stronger today; it's proof that you'll be even stronger tomorrow. So laugh like you mean it—because you do.

Turn the Mirror Back on You

I know signing divorce papers you never intended to have, while stepping on a Lego barefoot, and then reaching for the bottle of tequila only to realize it's empty, is the definition of "not great." But maybe the tips below will help turn your tragedy into a comedy.

1. Take a breath. Will this really matter a year from now? Or even next week? Most things that feel like full-blown disasters in the moment are about as heavy as a feather when you zoom out. Laugh at how ridiculous it is—and keep it moving. You've got bigger things to conquer.
2. When all else fails, try exaggerating the situation. "Yup, he left. One minute, we're discussing what to have for dinner, and the next, he's pulling a Houdini! Gone like socks in the dryer. At least give me the courtesy of a dramatic exit, you know? Maybe throw down some smoke bombs and run off into the sunset or something! What a loser." I swear, you'll crack yourself up.
3. Instead of spending time around too many wet blankets, surround yourself with people who can also laugh. They'll help you see the sunny side more easily. When you have friends who'll turn a funeral into a joke, it's hard not to join 'em: "I told my kids to play my Spotify playlist at my funeral. But only if they pay for premium. No one's sitting through ads at my send-off."

A Love Letter to Love

"Have enough courage to trust love one more time and always one more time."

—MAYA ANGELOU

Love in your second act can be complicated. It's like trying to navigate a rom-com written by someone who's had one too many espresso shots. Everyone's juggling six situationships, refining their Raya profiles, or still low-key texting their toxic ex because *closure* is a myth. But guess what? You, my queen, have hit the jackpot. You've found someone who doesn't make you want to fake a food allergy before the entrée arrives. It's like you've stepped into your own rom-com, and Hugh Grant just showed up with his floppy hair and awkward charm saying, "I'm just a boy, standing in front of a girl, asking her to love him." And you? You're ready to say, "Yes, you adorable disaster, let's go."

Cue the butterflies doing the cha-cha in your stomach, the goofy smiles that make you look like you've just discovered chocolate for the first time, and the endless replaying of your last conversation like it's your favorite Chappell Roan song on repeat. And let's not forget the *best* part—you're horny again! Turns out, the kids didn't completely drain you of your sexual appetite. Hallelujah! It's time to dust off the cobwebs and declare to the world your vagina is alive and thriving, ready to make its grand comeback. Move over, Renaissance—this is the Vaginaissance, and you're the star of the show.

When the Crush Is Cruuushhhhing

When we're in love, we're transported to our teen days, (sans acne) where our hearts are in our stomachs, and we get nervous any time we make eye contact with the object of our affection. The world is brighter, we think twice before skipping the gym, and food tastes better. Did Gordon Ramsay cook this?

Every time you and your beloved talk, you catch another detail—a laugh, a look, a tiny quirk, the same coffee order…oh my god, oh my god, oh my god, he's your soulmate.

This is also the phase where planning your imaginary future together becomes a part-time hobby. He likes dogs? Clearly, you're destined to get a golden retriever named Simba. He mentioned he's into hiking? Guess you're moving to Colorado! This is when love is *fun*.

And here comes the "L" word. Now, let me be clear: I've always been the "you say it first, or I'm taking that four-letter word to the grave" type. No way was I going to be the first to drop the L-bomb. But with one of my boyfriends, only two weeks in, those three little words were practically doing jumping jacks on the tip of my tongue, begging to be set free. So I let them out. I went all in and said it first. It took months before he finally said it back, but I didn't care—I felt like a legend for owning how I felt.

\So here's my advice, sister: If you feel those sparks, go all in. Say something. Don't let that feeling fizzle out like a sad bottle of champagne. Let it leap out of you like a confetti cannon at a surprise party. Life's way too short to keep the depths of your heart tucked away like a dusty secret in the attic. Playing by "the rules" is so last century. Love isn't meant to be boxed up and hidden; it's meant to break free, grab you by the hand, and drag you on the wildest, most unpredictable ride of your life. Let love give you wings, and watch yourself soar. That's what it's meant to do—so don't hold back. Fly, baby, fly.

Love Is Like a Houseplant

Once the object of your affection becomes permanent, you can't just water the relationship once and expect it to thrive like a low-maintenance succulent. It needs attention, care, and the occasional spritz of emotional Miracle-Gro. The good news? You don't need a grand romantic gesture or a couple's retreat in Bali. Small, intentional actions can keep your relationship fun and full of love.

Remember when you used to plan dates, wear real pants, and casually end up near their favorite coffee shop? Do that again! Surprise them with a planned night out—or even an at-home movie marathon without phones. Dressing up and giving each other uninterrupted attention can reignite the spark faster than a weekend getaway ever could.

Surprises don't have to be extravagant. It's the little things that keep love alive. Leave a sticky note in their bag that says, "Hope your Zoom meetings don't suck—love you!" or throw in a playful ass grab while making dinner. A hug, a handhold, or even a well-timed eyebrow raise across the room can remind you both that you're still very much in this together. Touch is like Wi-Fi for relationships: You don't realize how essential it is until you're disconnected.

Yes, there are the stale routines and moments where you wonder, "Is this still worth it?" But with patience, care, and the willingness to work through the mess, both can create something beautifully rewarding that only gets better with time. Feed it, nurture it, and watch it thrive.

It's a wild thing, that heart of yours—capable of big, messy, ridiculous love. So, own it, because being able to love is a superpower. And at the end of the day, it's not about him, anyway. It's about *you* and how you showed up bursting out like confetti making a giant sparkly mess.

Turn the Mirror Back on You

Look, sister, I get it. Every time you open your heart, you're taking a huge risk. The simple act of loving requires you to be brave. But if you choose to be vulnerable and love hard, it's worth every crazy minute.

1. Love makes you do things you'd never sign up for solo. You're an art nerd; he thinks Monet is a brand of pasta—but he's at The Getty grinning through it. He's an outdoorsy hiker; you'd rather binge *Love Is Blind*, but there you are—boots laced, trekking up hills you didn't know existed. Love yanks you out of your comfort zone

and drops you into someone else's world—with a front-row seat to experiences you never saw coming.

2. You get a PIC, a partner in crime, who'll follow you down any rabbit hole, no questions asked. Rearrange the furniture at 2:00 a.m.? They're lifting the couch half asleep. Feel like seeing the latest horror movie even though you'll be jumping out of your skin? They're putting their arms around you as you're clutching the bucket of popcorn. With the right person, even the smallest escapade feels like an epic adventure.
3. Love isn't always a walk in the park, and even if your relationship has an expiration date, it's those unexpected twists and turns that make it all worth it. From first dates that feel straight out of a reality show to road trips where neither of you thought to download the map, love gives you a highlight reel full of stories you'll be laughing about for ages. It's all those little fails and epic "oops" moments that make the journey legit. Because honestly, perfect is overrated, and a little mess is where all the real fun happens.

Manifestation Made Easy

"Whatever you hold in your mind on a consistent basis is exactly what you will experience in your life."

—THE MAN THAT CAN TURN YOU FROM "KIND OF HAPPY" TO A "FIRE-WALKING MILLIONAIRE," TONY ROBBINS

Alright, buckle up, buttercup, because it's time to enter one of my favorite topics: the wild world of manifestation. It's a word tossed around constantly by everyone, from the kiddies on social media to your local barista promising the oat milk latte is "manifesting good vibes." But what the hell does it mean, anyway? It's the practice of attracting your desires into reality through thoughts, beliefs, and actions. Sounds simple, right? Yup, about as simple as assembling IKEA furniture without the directions.

Manifesting is not just about scribbling "future billionaire" in your journal and expecting Jeff Bezos to invite you to the Amazon board of directors. No, manifesting is both an art and a science—a magical cocktail of vision, energy, and actual effort. You can't just sit around like Al Bundy, visualizing a perfect six-pack while munching on a bag of Flamin' Hot Cheetos, and expect abs to appear. I've tried. It doesn't work.

You must get really clear on what you want *first.* And then like a CEO walking into a boardroom *knowing* the deal's already sealed, you ask the universe for it with the utmost confidence, visualize it happening, and then walk forward with your day as if it's already happened!

But most of us have the attention span of a goldfish. We'll be visualizing our dream partner one minute and then spiraling into a stress-fueled panic about how our ex is probably thriving, or the massive credit card statement lurking in the mail, the next.

The mind loves drama, and it's a full-time job trying to keep it focused on the good stuff. You have to trick your brain into thinking you've already gotten what you want. Let's break it down step by step to turn you into a master manifester.

Step 1: Get Crystal Clear on What You Want

Manifestation starts with getting really, really clear about what you want. Like, clearer than glass, or your grandmother's unwanted opinions about your love life. You wouldn't walk into Starbucks and just say, "Surprise me!" You have a very specific order, and you get exactly what you ask for. The universe works the same way.

Let's say you want to manifest a relationship. Don't just say, "I want a boyfriend." The universe is going to be like, "OK, here's Chad from accounting, who smells like printer toner and will never remember your birthday." Nope. Be specific. "I want a loving, supportive, hilarious partner, five feet ten or taller, great teeth, who makes a killer breakfast." Now, *that* is manifesting with specificity.

Manifesting money? Imagine yourself holding a giant check, feeling the crisp paper between your fingers, the weight of all those zeros, and the giddy rush of financial freedom flooding your veins. The more vividly you can visualize and *feel* your future, the more your body goes, "Wait, is this real? Because it *feels* real." And your brain—sweet, loyal thing that it is—starts looking for ways to make that feeling match your reality. That's when opportunities show up. Ideas flow. Energy shifts.

Now, imagine treating your squad to a bougie dinner at that restaurant where the menu doesn't have prices (because if you have to ask, you can't afford it—except now you *can*). Hear the clink of champagne glasses, the roar of laughter, and the sound of your best friend saying, "You're literally the coolest person I know." Feel the smug satisfaction of paying the bill without even glancing at the total. Picture the serene calm that washes over you as you effortlessly pay your rent, credit card debt, *and* that random subscription you forgot you had. The goal is to make the dream so vivid, your nervous system starts adjusting *now* for what's coming. Make it so real you practically hear the *cha-ching* of your bank account updating in real time—that's how you get the universe vibing with you.

Scientific studies show that your brain is like that gullible friend who believes every wild story you tell her. It literally can't tell the difference between a real experience and one you've imagined. So, when you're sitting there imagining your dream partner, job, or financial success in vivid, swoon-worthy Technicolor detail, your brain is basically saying, "Whoa, this is happening right now!" and starts rewiring itself to get on board.

You're training your body to feel the high of your future success *before* it even shows up. It's like convincing your brain you're already living your best life—sipping mimosas in your dream house, wearing a silk robe, and yelling at your Roomba for missing a spot—even if, in reality, you're currently sitting on your couch in sweatpants, surrounded by three-day-old takeout containers and a cat that's judging your life choices. But here's the kicker: Your brain is like, "Oh, this is our life now? Cool, *let's act like it.*"

As a result, your behavior starts to shift. You begin making decisions and taking actions that align with that glittery, champagne-soaked future you've been visualizing. Maybe you finally update your resume, start that side hustle, or stop swiping left on people who look like they'd bring good vibes to a picnic. You're not just daydreaming anymore—you're *living* like the main character of your own rom-com, and the universe is taking notes.

And here's the science-y part to make you feel smart while you're manifesting: Your brain has these things called "mirror neurons," which basically say that "Fake it till you make it" is a legit strategy. When you vividly imagine yourself achieving your goals, these neurons fire up like they would if you were actually living that reality. It's like your brain is your hype squad going, "YES, WE'RE DOING THIS!" even if your current reality involves reheating pizza for the third time this week. Now, go forth and *cha-ching* your way to the life of your dreams. It's magic, bitches! Bippity-boppity-boo!

Step 2: Ask with Confidence

Now, here's where the fun really starts. You've gotta ask the universe with the kind of unshakable confidence that says, "Yes, I *know* I deserve this." The CEO walking into a boardroom, remember? Don't whisper. Don't hem and haw. Don't mumble. Don't second-guess yourself. Ask like someone who knows when they place their order, it's going to be perfect. Every. Single. Time. "I'll have a large iced latte, extra shot of espresso, one pump of vanilla—thank you very much." Not that sad, apologetic, "Um, hi, do you think maybe I could, like, possibly get a large iced latte? But *only* if you have time. And maybe, I don't know, a shot of espresso? But no pressure!"

Shit no, Sally! You need to be in your power! Be direct. Be unapologetic. The universe vibes off your frequency, so if you're giving off wishy-washy energy, don't be surprised if you get wishy-washy results. Put out that bold, confident ask, and watch what comes back to you. Bippity-boppity-boo.

Step 3: Visualize Like a Motherfucker

Visualization is the holy grail of manifestation. It's what bridges the gap between where you are now and where you want to be. A man whom I've spent countless hours studying, Dr. Joe Dispenza—manifestation guru and all-around smarty pants—talks a lot about "mental rehearsal." Mental rehearsal means closing your eyes and imagining yourself crushing your goals, feeling every detail like it's already happening, and engaging as many of your senses as possible. Is your dream home by the beach? Smell the ocean air, hear the waves crash onto the sand, and picture yourself on your balcony sipping your morning coffee and looking out on the water. What does the coffee taste like? Do you hear the sound of your children's laughter as they build sandcastles? And pay very close attention to how all of this makes you feel. Do you feel peaceful? Joyful? Confident? Empowered?

When you immerse yourself in these emotions, you're rewiring your brain. Neuroscience shows that your brain doesn't know the difference between imagining something and actually experiencing it, so your brain wires new neural circuits *as if that future is already happening.* You're teaching your body to feel the emotions of your future before it physically arrives. Bippity-boppity…you guessed it…boo.

Step 4: Take Inspired Action

Now, most people think they can just put the order out into the universe and then sit back, waiting for their dreams to just plop into their lap. Nope. Sorry. It requires action. Even people who won the lottery had to actually do something in order to win: get up, go to the store, choose the numbers, buy the ticket… you get the drift.

Manifesting is a dance between intention and action. But not just any action—*inspired action.* Inspired action comes from a place of alignment and intuition rather than from fear or obligation. It's the kind of action that feels right and effortless even if it requires work. It's fun work, not work-work. If you're manifesting a new job, you can't just light a candle and hope someone emails you an offer. You have to update your resume, network, and put yourself out there. The universe will meet you halfway, but you have to make the first move. Think of it as a cosmic partnership where you both do your part. If you're manifesting love, maybe that means saying yes to more social events.

If you're manifesting better health, it might mean actually using that gym membership you've been paying for since 2019.

As the Buddha with boobs, Dolly Parton, once said, "You can't just sit there and wait for people to give you that golden dream. You've got to get out there and make it happen for yourself." Do your part—set the intention, align your energy, and take inspired action—and trust the universe will do its part to support you.

Step 5: Let Go and Trust–Act as If It's Already Happened

Here's the part where most people hit a bump in the road: the whole letting go thing. To manifest your dream life, you've gotta loosen your grip on the how and when. If you're clinging to expectations like a dog with a bone, you're basically putting out vibes of desperation. It's like telling the universe, "Hey, I don't trust you to deliver," and that's a surefire way to keep your dreams juusssttt out of reach.

Look, I get it—waiting around for your dreams to come true is the worst, like planting seeds in your garden and then fighting the urge to dig them up every day to see if they've sprouted. But plants (and dreams) grow in their own time, not yours.

Here's the thing: The universe is smarter than all of us combined. Sometimes your manifestation doesn't show up right away because the stars haven't aligned yet. Or maybe, just maybe, the universe is cooking up something even better than what you asked for. If Wolfgang Puck was taking his time perfecting your gourmet meal, you wouldn't want him to rush and serve it undercooked, would you? Exactly. So, stop trying to micromanage the universe like a helicopter parent. Let go, trust the process, and keep your eyes on the prize. Stay present and keep your energy high-vibe. Because the more you convince yourself you're already winning, the closer you get to actually winning. And when it all comes together? That's when you'll realize you're not just manifesting—you're *manifeasting* on the fruits of your own badassery.

As they say, good things come to those who wait—and sometimes, the best things come when you least expect them.

Turn the Mirror Back on You

Homies, listen up! Let's get you waving your magic wand! If you're new to manifestation, there are some incredible teachers out there, some of whom I've personally worked with. You can contact them on Instagram and tell 'em I sent ya—@shannon.m.quinn is out of this world and changed me on a cellular level, and @spiritualactivator cleared my energy so quickly I started manifesting faster than a magician can pull a rabbit out of a hat. They have classes and lots of resources online. And here are some of my other favorites, whom you can also find online: Dr. Joe Dispenza, Abraham -Hicks, Bashar, and David Bayer. But in the meantime, let's get you started here.

1. What do you really want? Get super clear. Vague goals get vague results. Do you want a new job, a partner who actually texts back, or a dream vacation in Malta? Spell it out, down to the tiniest details.
2. Why do you want this? Is it for you, or are you trying to impress someone else? Be honest. The ego should not be in charge here. Your "why" should light you up like a neon sign. If your reason doesn't spark joy, rewrite it. You're not building a life for someone else's applause.

3. What limiting beliefs do you need to kick to the curb? Time to check the stories you're telling yourself. If you're thinking, *I'm not good enough* or *It's really hard to make money*, bye! We're not bringing that energy into the future. Those thoughts are expired, and your new reality doesn't have room for emotional clutter. Rewrite the script. Upgrade your mindset to "Money is really easy to make," or "Duh. Everything that I want, wants me back, because I'm worthy."
4. What steps can you take today to get closer to what you want? What's one small thing you can do now? Maybe you can send that email, sign up for that class, or finally update your LinkedIn profile.
5. Gratitude is a major vibe booster. Appreciate what you have now, and you'll make room for even more blessings. The universe responds to your *vibe*, not your thoughts. You can say, "I want abundance" all day long—but if your energy overall is screaming, "I'm desperate and nothing ever works out for me," that's the signal you're actually sending. Let the majority of your thoughts align with "Look at all this good shit I already have," and the universe is basically like, "Okayyy, I see you! Let's give her some more to brag about. "Gratitude is the universe's love language—lay it on thick, and it'll start spoiling you like a favorite child.

Marriage

"Before you marry someone, you should first make them use a computer with slow internet service to see who they really are."

—WILL FERRELL, KID FROM IRVINE, WHO WAS STREAKING IN THE MOVIE OLD SCHOOL. I WAS SITTING NEXT TO HIM, AND IT WAS AAAALLL OUT.

Ew, no! Gross! Fuck that shit! Do you like self-induced torture?! I'm joking. What I really mean to say is, "Congratulations! But are you out of your mind!?"

Alright, alright, jokes aside. So, you're ready to walk down the aisle, huh? Getting married is very romantic. It's a sparkly party with lots of dessert and questionable speeches that require courtesy laughs. But a wedding is a party that lasts one night while a marriage is an everyday journey, for as long as you both shall live. So, before you walk down that aisle, make sure you're not just signing up for the fantasy. Marriage is beautiful, yes, but it's also messy, hard, and requires both people to be fully in it, flaws and all. Your favorite divorcée is here to break it down for you, so that aisle doesn't feel like a plank.

Harry Fighting Styles

Let's talk about fighting styles, because trust me, everyone's got one. Are you the Hulk—flying into a rage over the tiniest thing, ready to smash furniture because someone left an empty toilet paper roll? Or maybe you're the Silent Assassin—the one who goes eerily quiet when you're mad, arms crossed, staring daggers, and waiting for your partner to miraculously "figure out" what they did wrong?

Neither of these approaches is winning you trophies for conflict resolution. If you're the Hulk, take a deep breath (or ten). If you're the Silent Assassin, here's a life-changing piece of advice you probably haven't heard since kindergarten: *Use your words!*

Relationships aren't a battleground. They're not about who can yell the loudest or out-sulk the other person. They're partnerships, and good ones require communication, not emotional warfare. Blowing up leaves you both exhausted and bitter, while shutting down turns every disagreement into a guessing game no one wants to play.

So, be honest with yourself: Can you fight fairly? Because the truth is, it's easy to be all lovey-dovey when everything's going great. But what about when things *don't* go your way? If you're already spotting red flags in the ways you handle conflict, trust me, those flags only get redder after marriage. Learning to fight fair now isn't just a nice idea—it's the glue that holds a lasting relationship together.

The Right Way to Wrangle

I don't care if you're sipping herbal tea from your zen garden while reading self-empowerment books in your meditation corner—if you're in a relationship, fights are going to happen. It's normal and nothing to shy away from when there's a clash of minds. But here's the million-dollar question: Can you fight respectfully, or are you going for the jugular every time? The health of a marriage is determined by how well you fight. Read that last sentence again. Fighting isn't the enemy of love; done right, it actually helps love grow.

Fighting fair means you're engaging in a real discussion, not entering a high-stakes game of who can hurl the most hurtful comments. Are you genuinely listening to your partner or just waiting for them to stop talking, so you can land your next emotional jab? Fighting fair is about staying true to the issue at hand without name-calling and without unearthing old grudges.

Remember, you're on the same team—it's not you versus them. You're not there to shatter their confidence; the goal is to resolve the problem, not to "win." And I get it—we're all tempted to toss out those zingers, but trust me, those cheap shots add up. Every time you attack them instead of the issue, you're chipping away at the respect and trust that hold your relationship together.

You're upset because they forgot date night? Great, talk about that. But don't drag in their messy college years or the time they forgot to buy your mom a birthday present back in 2019. That's just throwing fuel on the fire, and it'll get you nowhere.

You're both on the same side, which is that of peace and resolve. You're partners in life, not opponents in a boxing match. So, listen, slugger—don't deliver a verbal knockout just to feel victorious. Keep it classy. Keep it clean.

Compromise and Understanding

In a fight, you're both right! Yes, you heard me. Before you think I'm taking the easy way out, hear me out. You're both right because you're each coming to the argument with your own set of experiences and viewpoints. *Your opinion is valid from your perspective, and their opinion is valid from theirs.* It's pointless to try to convince someone that their perspective is wrong. It's like telling a dog not to chase a cat. It just doesn't compute.

The goal isn't to have a mic-drop moment where you annihilate your partner with indisputable truth bombs. This isn't a courtroom, and you're not auditioning for *Law & Order: Relationship Unit*. The goal is understanding each other's perspective and landing on…wait for it…dun, dun, dunnnnnn… compromise.

Compromise is the duct tape of love—it holds things together when tough conversations roll in. It's not about splitting everything fifty-fifty like you're divvying up gummy bears at recess. It's about finding middle ground where *both* of you feel seen and heard.

And it's not always "fair." Sometimes one person gives more this time, and the other steps up next time. Think of it like relationship yoga—flexible but balanced. If your partner wants to spend every weekend at their parents' house in Martha's Vineyard, but you'd rather have date nights, compromise could mean alternating weekends or setting aside specific "just us" time.

It's not about "winning" the argument or getting your way twenty-four seven—it's about making decisions where both of you feel valued. Because if one person's always "compromising" while the other's always cruising, that's not compromise—that's a compatibility issue…and honey, even I can't duct-tape that one together.

"I'm Sorry You Feel That Way..."

"I'm sorry you feel that way" is not an apology—it's deflecting responsibility and blaming the other person's feelings. A real apology means saying, "I messed up," and meaning it. It's not weakness—it's emotional strength. You're saying, "I'm sorry for my role in this"—and the most important part of an apology: You've gotta change after that. No magic tricks, just grown-up behavior.

And if you're the one accepting the apology? Don't let repeat offenders skate by. A mistake repeated multiple times isn't a mistake—it's a choice. Apologies only work when actions back them up. Otherwise, it's just lip service…and you deserve better.

The Deal-Breakers

Before you can waltz down Compromise Avenue, you need to get familiar with your non-negotiables—your deal-breakers. Think of these as the boundaries that are set in stone—those areas where bending would feel like breaking. They're the hills you're willing to die on. This isn't something to figure out in the heat of the moment when you're debating whose turn it is to do the dishes. It's something you should reflect on when you're calm, centered, and ideally holding your favorite latte. For some, it's about the big stuff: financial responsibility, loyalty, religious affiliation, or the desire to have kids. For others, it might be something that seems small to outsiders but feels huge to you, like the way your partner shows affection or respects your family traditions. They are deeply personal, and there's no right or wrong answer. But you must be honest with yourself.

For me, my non-negotiables are my children. My partner must realize and accept that my children come first. There's no negotiating that. Period. Like, if you want to plan a spontaneous vacation, and it conflicts with my son's soccer game or my daughter's ballet recital, sorry, but that's a hard no. And if you try to tell me how to mother my children? Bless your heart.

Love Is a Choice, Not Just a Vibe

Love is this magical feeling that hits you every morning like the smell of morning dew. Ha! That's the best damn joke in this book. No, sis, love is a choice you make every single day.

Some days love is as smooth as a Sunday brunch mimosa. But then...there are...other days. The days where you're so annoyed with them that you're practically Googling "how to disappear and start a new life in Bali." When your routine has set in, mystery is out the door, and they leave their clothes next to the hamper instead of in it. (That's the kind of partner I call "the almost done." You ask him to take the trash out, and he leaves it by the door, or right outside the door. And does he replace the liner? Hell no! Everything is always "almost done.").

You see, love isn't always a given. It's an active, conscious decision. You're choosing to be there, choosing to stay, even though you're one "Where are my keys?" away from packing a suitcase. As a couple, you can either grow together or grow apart. Either way, you *will* grow.

You're not just saying, "I love you" on the good days; you're saying, "I'm choosing you" even on the tough days. If you're not ready to choose them on the hard days, the "Seriously, can you chew any louder?" days, then it might be time to rethink the whole matter.

If you're expecting love to be this constant fairy-tale feeling, you're gonna be disappointed. Love is both champagne and cold leftovers. It's date nights and awkward silences. It's fireworks and flat tires. It's the "Nothing in my closet fits" days, the "Why is this happening to me?" days. Find someone who isn't fazed by the messy, unfiltered, real-life stuff. Because real love isn't afraid of a little chaos. Marriage isn't about perfection; it's about persistence. And if you can choose each other even when the trash is "almost done," and you're one eye roll away from checking flights to Bali, then maybe you're on to something.

Turn the Mirror Back on You

Listen, boo-bear, no one gets married planning their divorce. Before you take that trip down the aisle, ask yourself these questions to make sure this is what you truly want. And if you realize it isn't, know that it's perfectly OK to call off the big day. This is your life, your forever, and only you have the right to decide what that forever should look like.

1. Do you have aligned values and life goals, or are you hoping it'll sort itself out? Because if one of you wants to live off-grid in a yurt, and the other wants a penthouse in New York City, you might need more than positive vibes to make that work.
2. I cannot stress this enough: *The health of a relationship is determined by how you handle conflict.* Are you comfortable with how you handle your fights? If your style is quiet while your partner makes it seem like they're on an episode of *Jerry Springer*, you may want to have a look at that.
3. Do you want to high-five them more than you want to fuck them? If your love language looks similar to the one you have with your brother, you have a problem.

4. Can you accept this person's flaws, and can they accept yours, or do you fantasize about changing them like an HGTV makeover? If you're hoping marriage will magically cure their drinking habit, or a baby will make things better, you're wrong.
5. Do you feel respected and valued, or do you have to remind them every week that you're not their personal assistant? You deserve to be treated like the royalty you are, not like Alexa.
6. Do you see yourself growing old with this person, or will you be hiding their dentures out of revenge? Looks fade, and you'll have phases where life may pull you in and out of love, but at the end of the day, are you proud to be theirs? If you can imagine laughing together through wrinkles and orthopedic shoes, then you're probably good to go.

No

"I said no."

—ELLE WOODS, LEGALLY BLONDE, IN THE BEST SCENE IN THE MOVIE WHEN PROFESSOR CALLAHAN MAKES A PASS AT HER, AND SHE FINALLY PUTS HER FOOT DOWN

Alright, sunshine, let's talk about the mighty, magical, and terrifying word: "no." It's simple, but saying it can feel like committing a social crime. Toddlers scream "NO!" without a second thought, but grown-ass women? We hem, haw, and guilt-trip ourselves into saying "Suuuure" when our gut is yelling "FUCK NO!" Like when your neighbor asks you to join their essential oils group "just to see if it's a good fit," and you're like, "I barely have time to shower, Linda, let alone sell lavender moon juice on Facebook Live." Hard. Fucking. No. Will someone be disappointed? Absolutely. Is disappointment a part of life? Absolutely. *Every time you say "yes" to something you don't want to do, you're saying "no" to yourself*—and that's a one-way ticket to Resentmentville, where you'll be stuck hosting a pity party for one.

If you want to make room for the full-body "fuck yes" moments that light you up like the Fourth of July, you've got to stop crowding your calendar with half-hearted obligations. "No" is the major life flex you need to master.

Your Energy Bank Account

Picture your energy as a bank account. Every time you say "yes" to something that drains you, you're making a withdrawal. And when you run out of energy funds, you're left overdrafted, exhausted, and lying in bed at 2:00 a.m. wondering why you agreed to help your friend set up for her cousin's daughter's one-year birthday party.

Saying "no" to people who don't deserve your time or energy is a crucial part of self-love. This was something I had to learn the hard way. And as Brené Brown said, "Daring to set boundaries is about having the courage to love ourselves, even when we risk disappointing others." Mic drop.

You can't show up as the badass you are if you're running on empty because you said "yes" to every coffee date, work favor, and emotional vampire in your life. Protect your energy like it's a winning lottery ticket. Now, our opposite gender is masterful at this. God bless 'em, but guys have no problem dropping one-liners like "nope" or "can't" without a single ounce of explanation. Meanwhile, we women tie ourselves into a pretzel trying to accommodate other people's needs.

If you've got little ones who are basically mini yous running around and soaking up your every move, then modeling the power of "no" is even more important. I've got two boys and a girl who love to roughhouse like it's WWE in my living room, so I've made sure they're absolute pros at "no." When one of them calls a time-out, the others stop immediately—no questions asked. No negotiations. Game's over.

It's totally OK to throw up the stop sign and say, "I've had enough." "No" is a boundary, plain and simple, and the other person has to respect it even if it cramps their vibe.

I Am the Boss of Me

We've all been there—tempted by something that sounds amazing but feels totally off. Like a dinner invite when all you really need is Netflix, wine, and zero human interaction. Or you go on a date with a guy who could be the one and afterward he texts, "I think I could really see myself falling in love with you. What are your thoughts on joint bank accounts?"

Fuck no. Sir, I just learned your middle name. Please back away from my finances *and* my nervous system.

Saying "no" isn't selfish—it's a power move. Steve Jobs famously said you have to say "no" to the things that don't matter to focus on what does. Be the CEO of your life. Choose your commitments wisely—if it doesn't spark joy or align with your goals, pass.

Just because something looks good on paper doesn't mean it's right for you. Saying "no" to the wrong things creates space for the right things.

Hold Out for the Cake

Sometimes the universe serves up "opportunities" that are about as appealing as a soggy salad. And sure, you're tempted to say *yes* because you're scared it's the best you'll ever get—don't. You're not here to date the human equivalent of a plain rice cake just because you're pushing forty and terrified of being alone. Or to stay in that low-paying job simply because all your friends are there.

Raise. Your. Standards.

If fear is calling the shots, then you're surrendering. You weren't put on this planet to collect crumbs and pretend it's a feast. Stop accepting bare-minimum energy from people, jobs, or situations that should've been left on read.

The universe actually *loves* it when you know your worth. Saying *no* to mediocrity is the ultimate power move. It's like telling the universe, "Cute try, but I'm holding out for the good stuff. Try again."

Think of the universe as your personal cosmic concierge—it's constantly rearranging things behind the scenes. But when you settle for crumbs, you're basically announcing you don't think you deserve the whole damn cake.

Hold out for the cake. It's coming. And it's all yours.

Turn the Mirror Back on You

Need help flexing your "no" muscle? Let's dive in—because mastering "no" is the first step to unlocking your best "YES."

1. Before you hit 'em with a "yes," check in with your body. Got a lump in your throat? Heart racing? That weird cold, numb feeling? Yeah, that's your inner wisdom screaming "NOOOO!" We've been taught to think with our heads, but your body's like a built-in BS detector. Listen to it—it'll never steer you wrong.

2. Context matters. "No" is a complete sentence, but you can still be thoughtful. If you can't do dinner with your friend after a tough day because you're this close to a mental breakdown, try: "I'm tapped out right now, but I care about what you're going through. Can we catch up in a few days?" It's not about over-explaining—it's about keeping the connection real when it counts.
3. If saying "no" makes you sweat, ask yourself why. Are you a people-pleaser? Do *you* secretly get salty when someone tells you "no"? If someone guilts or shames you for setting a boundary, that's a them problem, not a you problem. Time to flex those "ovaries of steel" and put yourself first. Prioritizing your peace isn't selfish—it's essential.

Now

"One of the most tragic things I know about human nature is that all of us tend to put off living. We are all dreaming of some magical rose garden over the horizon—instead of enjoying the roses that are blooming outside our windows today. Why are we such fools—such tragic fools?"

—DALE CARNEGIE, A REALLY SMART GUY

The eternal now. The right-this-second palooza. Otherwise known as the present moment. You don't have an hour ago, and you're not even promised five minutes from now, just the time it takes to read this line right here. The only place the past and the future reside is in your head. The more you can stay rooted in the present, the happier you'll be.

It's Not Your Fault

From the moment our first armpit hair appears, someone sits us down and says, "So, Sally…you're about to embark on a major milestone here. Turning ten ain't for pussies. Time to start thinking about what you want to be when you grow up."

"I don't have a fucking clue, Uncle Chris. I'm still trying to figure out why I have hair growing in places it has no business growing."

It's not our fault we turn into adults who spend half our day thinking about everything except what we're actually doing. Our brains are basically on permanent scroll mode—complaining about what we don't have, obsessing over what we want, or spiraling into random thoughts: "What should I make for Christmas dinner next year? Do penguins have knees??"

But there are joys in the present moment that get missed because we're so busy trying to catch the greased pig in our minds. You're allowed to take a breath. You *should* sit and enjoy your mid-afternoon latte. Don't be forever on the hustle train. Get off every now and then and notice the small beauties right in front of you: the smell of freshly laundered clothes, a great hair day for no reason, the sun bursting through the clouds on a misty morning.

The children will not starve if you don't occupy your mind with your mental grocery list right this second. Breathe into the now, and you might actually see you already have everything you need, right in front of you.

Turn the Mirror Back on You

Time traveling is exhausting. It's OK to daydream or reminisce, but when you're living inside the restrictive walls of your mind, life becomes a lot more stressful. Try some of the things below to get you out of your head and into the daily glories right in front of your nose.

1. Take a walk in Mother Nature. Everything happens in real time. Flowers bloom, birds chirp, leaves rustle—and none of it's waiting for you to stop doom-scrolling. You can only notice these little miracles if you're actually present.
2. Check yourself: Is whatever you're obsessing over actually necessary? Are you still replaying that awkward convo from weeks ago or stressing about what your kid's teacher thinks of you? Or worse—spiraling over future what-ifs you can't control? Stop. You're wasting prime mental real estate on things that don't matter. Free up your brain for stuff that does. You've got better things to do.
3. Meditate. Just five to ten minutes can work actual magic on your brain. You don't need a monk on speed dial. Just breathe. Inhale for four counts, exhale for six. Repeat ten times. Boom—you're basically a mindfulness ninja. It's the fastest way to shut up the mental chaos and actually slow the fuck down long enough to smell those proverbial roses.

Orgasms

"Oh my god, oh my god, yes, yes, yes!"

—ALMOST EVERY PERSON ON THE PLANET BETWEEN THE AGES OF SEVENTEEN AND SEVENTY (GIVE OR TAKE)

I didn't fully get the power of female sexual empowerment until *Sex/Life* exploded. Over 160 million people tuned in to watch me as Billie, navigating mind-blowing fictional sex and all the messy, real-life stuff every woman can relate to. There was something for everyone—I was either crying or masturbating in every scene. Relatable right?

After the show premiered, what hit me the hardest was learning how many women have never experienced an orgasm. Studies show that up to half of women aren't satisfied with how often they reach that biological imperative. Sis, let me be the first to tell you—orgasms are more than seven seconds of euphoria. They're the ultimate power-up. I'm not just talking about pussy power (although, yes); it's the way you show up in life. Owning your pleasure impacts how you walk into a room, how you take up space, how you radiate confidence without even trying. After years of extensive personal research (you're welcome), I've realized that embracing your sexuality is like unlocking the cheat code to your best self. It's the swagger in your step, the sparkle in your eye, and that glow-up energy that makes people wonder what your secret is. Spoiler: It's you. Turn yourself on—and light up the world.

Orgasms Are Retinol for Our Bodies

Our climax is so much more than eight thousand nerve endings throwing a party. And by that, I don't mean whether you're a yeller or the silent type. Your "sonic landscape" can change by the day. One minute you're a breathy, Sabrina Carpenter sex kitten, the next you're dropping F-bombs like a sailor on shore leave. Pleasure isn't one-size-fits-all; it's a custom playlist, and every hit is a banger. Pun definitely intended.

But let's be clear: Female orgasms aren't just fun—they're functional. They're the ultimate wellness hack. Need to relax? It's stress relief on steroids. Can't sleep? It's basically organic melatonin. Want better skin? Orgasms boost estrogen, which cranks up your collagen production. It's a literal facelift—no wonder NARS named a blush after it. That post-sex glow? It's real. Dewy, glowy, sex skin is nature's way of saying, "Keep up the good work."

So, let me prescribe you the best form of self-care there is: your pleasure. And if you're currently riding solo? Who cares! Grab a vibrator, dildo, or whatever makes your clit sing—and start rubbing—doctor's orders.

Turn the Mirror Back on You

Never had an orgasm before? No biggie! Consider this your official intro to your new favorite hobby. Let's get you on the Pleasure Express—you're about to unlock a whole new world.

1. Don't overthink it. Forget chasing the "big O" and focus on what feels good. Explore what turns you on even if you've never climaxed. If partners haven't cracked the code, learn your own map first—then teach them the highlights. Flying solo? Sex toys are game-changers. Need inspo? Check out OMGyes.com—it's basically Pleasure 101 but way more fun.
2. Notice how you feel after an orgasm. Are you feeling feisty? Playful? Like you could conquer the world and charm the barista with a single glance? *That's primal you.* No wrong answers here—just pure, unfiltered confidence. Tap into that glow and let it spill into your everyday vibe. You're that girl—own it.

Outlaw

"Here's to the crazy ones. The misfits. The rebels. The troublemakers. The round pegs in the square holes. The ones who see things differently.... You can quote them, disagree with them, glorify or vilify them. About the only thing you can't do is ignore them. Because they change things.... And while some may see them as the crazy ones, we see genius. Because the people who are crazy enough to think they can change the world, are the ones who do."

—STEVE JOBS, LISA'S DAD

I got sent to the principal's office a lot when I was a kid. And not because I was doing something cool, like sneaking smokes or running a black-market candy ring. Nope—I was there for the heinous crime of *talking too much.*

The teacher would ask a question, and if she didn't call on me fast enough, I'd blurt out the answer before anyone else could even inhale. I couldn't keep my trap shut. Fuck, I was annoying. Kids would hiss, "Hey, Sarah, you're so far up the teacher's ass, you've got some brown on your nose."

But here's the scoop—I wasn't trying to be a teacher's pet. I just didn't get why I had to wait for *permission* to share my thoughts. Like, hold the phone, Mrs. Bellamy—you mean to tell me I stayed up all night highlighting every damn fact about the American Revolution, and now I have to sit here with my hand in the air like a well-behaved Victorian orphan *waiting* for you to call on me in order to speak? Make it make sense.

So off I'd march to the principal's office, chin up and righteous, declaring, "What about women's lib? Free speech? All the badass women who fought so I could have a voice? You can't silence me! Give me liberty or give me death!"

Sure, I was a tiny drama queen with a big mouth—but after spending most of junior high scrubbing chalkboards, I finally got the hint. For a while, anyway.

Rules, Like a Salad Buffet, Are Boring

My rebellion didn't clock out after junior high detention—it followed me straight into my career, much to the despair of my representatives. Not because I was still a blabbermouth (though, fair), but because I treated "the rules" of the entertainment industry like they were optional fine print.

When *This Is Us* hit the airwaves, it didn't just touch my soul—it full-on hugged it. I was obsessed. The writing, the emotion, the raw, messy beauty of real human connection—it cracked me wide open in the best way. So, I called my agents and said, "Whatever it takes, please get me on this show." Their response? "Tough luck, kid. All the roles are taken."

Bull. Shit.

When something lights you up that much, you don't just walk away—you kick the damn door off its hinges. I felt this show in my bones, and come hell, high water, or Hollywood politics, I was going to get in front of those producers somehow. If the universe wasn't going to hand me an opportunity, I'd rip one out of its stingy little hands. So, I did what any rational, rule-breaking actor would do: I went rogue. I found the email address of the creator, Dan Fogelman, and sent him a message that was equal parts fan mail and desperate plea. I gushed about his writing and said I'd do *anything* to be on the show—even if it meant warming up his coffee or color-coordinating his sock drawer.

Now, this is a big no-no in the entertainment industry. Actors have representation for a reason. It's to filter out all the trash and to make sure all the incoming/outgoing phone calls are legit. But that show was a buzz in my veins I couldn't ignore. I told my reps what I had done, in true "whoops—my bad" fashion, and they were gobsmacked

"You did *what*?! There's protocol! That's what you have agents for. You're not ever supposed to reach out to producers directly!" they yelled, insisting I'd blown my shot at him ever hiring me. But almost ten years later, I proved them wrong. I got an audition for another one of his shows, *Paradise*. I walked into the audition room, and the first thing he says is, "Sarah Shahi. You wrote me an email years ago, and I never forgot it. I'm so excited to finally meet you." I did my thing, and Dan hired me. And I never had to warm his coffee or coordinate his socks.

Now let's dive into the *Sex/Life* audition, which was basically a masterclass in "Come as you are, yogurt stains and all." The role was for a tired, stay-at-home mom who couldn't stop daydreaming about her wilder days. Now, in Hollywood, even "Homeless Girl #1" is expected to show up with perfect beachy waves and a full face of contouring. So, naturally, a "tired mom" would probably be played by someone who looks like she just stepped out of a spa, right?.

Not me.

I showed up looking like I'd just been hit by a truck full of toddlers—having four-year-old twins, at the time, was basically the same thing. I walked into the audition room wearing pajamas, a knotted ponytail that hadn't seen a brush in days, and what I'm pretty sure was dried yogurt on my sweater (breakfast? snack? art project? who knows). Concealer? Nah. I barely had the energy to find my pants, let alone my makeup bag.

The producers looked at me like I'd just crawled out of a laundry hamper. One of them even handed me a brush—bless their heart—but I politely declined. I didn't want to play some glossy, Instagram-filtered version of motherhood. I wanted to show the raw, real, *exhausted* truth of it. Because let's be real, moms don't have time for perfect hair. We're too busy keeping tiny humans alive and wondering if we've eaten anything besides graham crackers.

It worked! I booked the job. Sometimes, the best way to nail an opportunity is to show up as your authentic, yogurt-stained self. So, ladies, whether you're walking into an audition, a boardroom, or just another day of mom life, remember this: You don't have to be perfect. You just have to be *you. Be an outlaw for yourself.* Be your own damn revolution.

And look, sister, sometimes I did "me" and didn't end up getting the job. But I have no regrets because I was authentic to who I am. I didn't let my vision be compromised. I didn't let the opinions of others tell me I couldn't do or be something- because success isn't about following the rules. It's about staying true to who you are along the way. Regardless of the outcome, you will always win. At the end of the day, the only rule that matters is the one you make for yourself. And that, my friends, is how you win—even if you're wearing pajamas.

Set a "Bad" Example

At thirteen, Joan Jett was gifted her first guitar and started taking lessons. Her teacher—apparently stuck in the Stone Age—told her girls could only play folk music. Her response? A big ol' "fuck off," followed by teaching herself how to rock. From that moment on, she was defying the norm: a rebel *with* a cause and a killer guitar riff. She wasn't just the first of her kind in a male-dominated industry—she was a force of nature.

When no label would take her on, she said, "Fine, I'll do it myself," co-founded her own label, and sold records out of the trunk of her car. Then she released "I Love Rock 'n' Roll," and it hit #1 on the Billboard charts, staying there for seven weeks. The same labels that turned her down probably choked on their cigar smoke. If she'd played by the industry's rules, we'd have missed out on the godmother of punk.

Then there's Rosa Parks, the ultimate outlaw for justice. With one quiet yet powerful act—refusing to move to the back of the bus—she sparked a revolution that transformed the oppressive system of racial segregation. She didn't need a guitar or a stage to make history; she just needed the courage to say, "No more." Both women, in their own ways, rewrote the rules and changed the world. Because sometimes, breaking the rules isn't just an option—it's a necessity.

"Bad" girls really do make history. It's been proven time and time again. Entire books have been written about the women who were brave enough to defy the odds. Marie Curie, Sojourner Truth, Frida Kahlo, Dolly Parton, Serena Williams, and more have proven that it pays to be an outlaw for your dreams.

So, sis, be rebellious in a world that's constantly trying to get you to conform. Stick to your guns, and your values, like glue. Be brave enough to color outside the lines and zig-zag outside the box. Trust that your wild ideas are worth pursuing, even when they scare you. Let your ambition be louder than other people's doubts. Speak up, even if it's not your turn. Tear up the rulebook and dance in its confetti. Make a little trouble out there—and make it on behalf of women everywhere.

Turn the Mirror Back on You

Believing in yourself ain't for sissies. It's a radical act of self-love, and most people need some practice.

1. Ask yourself, "Why do I believe in this?" What is driving your passion? Are you inspired by personal thoughts, or are you jumping on the bandwagon? Either way, understanding your emotions will strengthen your conviction.
2. What does success look like to you? For me, I learned the hard way that changing myself to fit what someone else wanted never felt right. Even if I got the job, something always felt off. So, I made a decision: *Success isn't booking the gig—it's showing up as me.* If I present myself exactly as I am, no filter, then I've already won. Getting the gig? That's just the cherry on top. There is no price I'm willing to pay in exchange for my beliefs.

3. What are you willing to sacrifice to be successful? Are you ready to give up time, comfort, and maybe even stability to pursue your dreams? Success isn't served on a silver platter—it's built with sleepless nights and saying "no" to what's easy, so you can say "yes" to what's worth it. Big wins require bold moves.
4. Are you ready for some people to throw shade your way, or should we grab some sunscreen before you step into the ring? When you decide to color outside the box of conformity, not everyone is going to agree with you. And that's OK! The only person who needs your approval is you.

Pain: Your Annoying Life Coach

"Bring your attention to the pain as if you were gently comforting a child, holding it all in a loving and soothing attention."

—JACK CANFIELD, ZEN DADDY WHO CO-AUTHORED THE CHICKEN SOUP FOR THE SOUL SERIES

Pain is a fucking pain in the ass.

From the time you had your first ouchie, your mommy did anything to make the pain go away: kiss it and make it better, put a Mickey Mouse Band-Aid on it, maybe even give you a double-scooped ice-cream cone. You were taught that pain is "bad."

We run from it, hide, look for healing at the bottom of a bottle. Personally, my forte was drowning it with alcohol and sugar then crying when no one was looking. Shocking that didn't work out for me long term. Everyone wants to avoid it, numb it, or outrun it like they're in a marathon sponsored by denial. But here's the truth: Pain isn't your enemy. It's that no-nonsense life coach you didn't ask for but desperately need.

Think of your pain like a howling storm. At first, your impulse is to run and seek cover, but if you give yourself just a few moments of standing in its center, you'll see its purpose is not to destroy everything in sight but to actually cleanse you—to realign you with the path you're *meant* to be on. You can't put a Mickey Mouse Band-Aid on a relationship that's not working. You can't expect a double-scooped ice-cream cone to make your boss more human (well, strike that—it *could* work for, like, five minutes). There's no more "kiss it and make it better" when you're an adult. You have to invite your pain into the most sacred chambers of your heart and trust that it won't break you; it will build you.

Beauty in the Bruise

After almost a decade of floating through life like a wet noodle—limp, directionless, and utterly uninspired—I stumbled upon a quote by Pema Chödrön that stopped me in my tracks: "Instead of asking ourselves, 'How can I find security and happiness?' we could ask ourselves, 'Can I touch the center of my pain?'"

Whoa, lady. I don't care if you're a Buddhist nun with a direct line to enlightenment. For years, I'd been running from my pain like it was an ex I spotted at the grocery store. Avoidance was my superpower. I dodged, I distracted, I numbed—anything to keep from facing the ache that had taken up permanent residence in my chest. And now you're telling me I should *touch* it? Like, willingly? No thanks.

But here's the thing: No matter how fast I ran, the pain kept showing up like an unpaid bill. It was always there, lurking in the background, waiting for me to slow down long enough to notice it. I was stuck in the hurt locker for so long, I thought, *What do I have to lose?*

I closed my eyes, quieted the world around me, and took a deep breath. A few minutes later, there it was—my pain. Not as some vague, shadowy concept, but as a tangible presence, sitting right in the center of my heart. It was like a black hole, sucking in all the love, joy, and light I carried. It was heavy, dark, and terrifying. But instead of running, I did something radical: I spoke to it.

"Why are you here?" I asked. "What are you trying to tell me?"

I sat with it for days, getting acquainted with it as if it were a long-lost friend. No distractions, no pretending I was fine. I journaled like a novelist on a deadline, pouring out every angry, sad, and confused thought.

And then it hit.

There was no blame, no dramatic finger-pointing—just truth. I wanted to feel like the main character of my life, not some background extra quietly folding laundry. Pretending that the life I was living was the one I wanted had become exhausting, like wearing heels two sizes too small—I could fake it for a while, but once I "touched the center of my pain," eventually, I couldn't pretend any longer. That raw truth became the fire that propelled me towards my divorce. I played the role of domestic housewife for about three more months—one last season of sorting socks and folding fitted sheets—and then, the curtain fell. My time in that role had officially come to an end.

As Rumi said, "The wound is the place where the light enters you." My heartbreak cracked me wide open, and in its place, something stronger grew—someone who knows her worth, sets her standards, and no longer apologizes for having high expectations.

Accepting my pain was the hardest thing I had ever done—but it transformed me. So, the next time life smacks you with a curveball, don't be a ninny—catch it. Let it knock you down if it must, but rise again, stronger, wiser, and jump into the life you're meant to live.

Turn the Mirror Back on You

I know it's much easier to drown our pain with distractions than it is to confront them. But when you're ready to view your pain as a *teacher*, you'll see everything you've ever wanted is on the other side.

1. Allow yourself to *really* feel what's going on. Take a few minutes out of your day. Whether you cry, journal, or scream, you're feeling something because it's meant to come out, so get curious about it. Resisting will only make it worse. Experience it. Whether or not you take action on it, sitting with it will make you feel better.
2. Be kind to yourself. You don't need to stay in your pain. Just like everyone else on this planet, you're doing the best you can. Give yourself some compassion, maybe a self-care activity. Whatever you do, acknowledge it without judgment.
3. Try to literally touch your pain. See if you can locate it in your body. Does it feel like a lump in your throat? Maybe you need to speak up. Mine was in my heart,

and I knew exactly what that meant. I was betraying myself. Put your hand over the area of discomfort and give it lots of love.

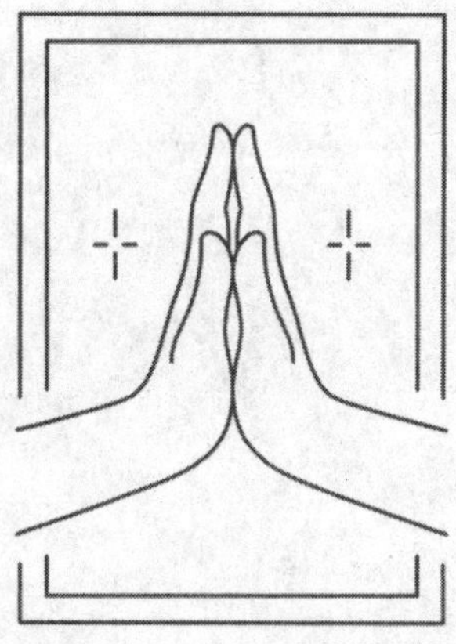

4. Breathe through your discomfort. Don't try to change it. The average time we feel the intensity of an emotion is only ninety seconds before it shifts into something else.

Progesterone

"Progesterone is the OG of all hormones, the MVP of your body. When it's low, you're screwed."

—ME

Are you bloated? Unhappy? Does your vagina feel like a sand dune? Do you put down more food than a garbage disposal? Well, sister, maybe you're lacking the happy hormone! I ain't talking dopamine or serotonin. I mean progesterone!

Right after my forty-first birthday, I woke up and didn't recognize the body I was living in. I was carrying an extra seven pounds, my jeans were holding on for dear life, and my fork had zero brakes. Mentally? I was a burrito of depression wrapped in a blanket of crankiness.

For months, I dieted, exercised, got the recommended eight hours of sleep, and nothing budged. I felt so out of sorts that I went to my doctor. He did a hormone panel, and—TADA!

There it was: low progesterone! I was missing the main ingredient that regulated all these functions! No wonder I felt like a soggy sock all the time.

A prescription later, I'm thrilled to report that my appetite changed. I dropped the excess weight. My vagina became a waterfall, and the pep in my step was back. Progesterone stabilized my moods, decreased my stress, and made me snooze like Sleeping Beauty. It was the ultimate serenity serum. I went from a ball of anxiety to a Zen master.

Why am I telling you this? Because it's our responsibility as part of the sisterhood to talk about these things! Progesterone is certainly not commercialized. We're quicker to advertise Prozac than we are progesterone. And society has us conditioned into thinking it's taboo to discuss the biological changes we miracle-makers of the world go through, yet Viagra, a pill that makes a limp dick hard, rolls off everyone's tongue.

So, sis, if you're feeling out of sorts, I want you to know you're not going nuts! You just need a hormone panel from your doctor—and just maybe, you need to hop on the P-wagon! Progesterone's the glue that holds your sanity, mood, and metabolism together. It has changed my life, and every woman needs to know about it. Get some of that Zen master juice and go back to being the fierce queen you know yourself to be.

Turn the Mirror Back on You

I'm no doctor (although I may play one on TV—oh, come on, I had to say that), but ask yourself if you're experiencing any of the following:

1. Do you have irregular periods? Mine started changing after forty. Progesterone regulated them.

2. Do you have difficulty falling or staying asleep?
3. Is your libido low? Low progesterone can result in a reduced sex drive, and you're way too young to not feel hot and horny!
4. Are you constantly fatigued? This was a big indicator for me. No matter how much sleep I got, or how easy the day was, I was moving about as fast as a rock. You deserve better. Consult with your doctor, get on the P, and watch your life change!

Quality Time (With You)

"Almost everything will work again if you unplug it for a few minutes, including you."

—ANNE LAMOTT, AUTHOR OF ONE OF MY FAVES, BIRD BY BIRD

I'm forty-three years old. Do you wanna know the last time I took a trip somewhere by myself? Without kids or a partner? TO THE BATHROOM LAST NIGHT. Every getaway I'd ever been on came with kids, work, or a partner in tow. But finally, it was time to make a bold move for some quality time with *me*. So last summer, I packed an overnight bag, kissed the chaos goodbye, and jetted off to Colorado to soak up some mountain magic and get in some quality time with my healer. (We've been over this. Yes, I have a healer. I live in LA. Gimme a break.)

At first, the space to be with myself felt unusual. You mean I don't have to fry bacon to crispy perfection in the morning?

I don't have to think about soccer practices and spilled juice boxes? What do I even do? Whatever the fuck I want! It was the freest I've felt since that time I ran away from home at fourteen (my mom found me two hours later—so much for rebellion).

The weekend was spent with a stack of books and a bottle (or three) of wine and a few friends. It was *freedom* with a capital F. I hiked in the crisp mountain air, stargazed like a dreamy poet, and slept in like it was my job. Somewhere in there, I found "me." The me who laughs too loud, makes slightly off-color jokes that would scandalize the PTA, stops to have full-on conversations with squirrels, and blasts country music while ordering room service at midnight like it's my birthright. The version of me who double-texts her friends, does a little two-step while brushing her teeth, and believes that pancakes and prosecco are a perfectly respectable dinner. The *me* I'd nearly forgotten under all the to-do lists and juice boxes.

Two nights later, I was a new woman. I hit the reset button in a way I never had before. I was ready to go back to cutting crusts off sandwiches and finding lost shoes. And maybe, I'd even keep a little bit of her with me when I got home.

Every woman deserves to feel like the star of her own getaway story, if even just for a couple of days. How are you supposed to be the badass boss or supermom if you're running on empty? *You're worth the trip.*

We've been conditioned to think that every moment needs to be productive. I can't tell you how many women I've talked to who say, "When I have time to myself, I get so antsy. I feel like I should be doing something." Instead of basking in the art of doing nothing, we start deep-cleaning the grout or reorganizing our closets.

Maybe you just want to chill with a cup of tea and watch the world go by. Perhaps catching up on your fave podcast or binge-watching *Nobody Wants This* is what you need to unwind. Whatever it is, take a break and do you!

The most productive thing you can sometimes do is absolutely nothing. Quality time with yourself is about reconnecting with who you are outside of all the roles you play for other people. It's about shutting off the noise—both external and internal—and tuning into what you actually want and need.

In this world where we're bombarded with more information than a *Jeopardy!* contestant on a hot streak, it's crucial to give our hearts a little airtime. But don't stress—you don't have to book a week-long silent retreat in Malta or hide out in a cabin for days. It can be as simple as turning off your notifications, grabbing your keys, and going on a choose-your-own-adventure drive. Let the road signs guide you and go wherever the wind takes you. Enjoy the journey, see what surprises pop up, and for once, don't pressure yourself to know the final destination.

Because life is messy and magical, and sometimes the best way to make sense of it is to roll down the windows, blast your favorite song, and just flow.

Turn the Mirror Back on You

All of us could use some downtime to be with our number-one neglected bestie: our own self. At first, it might feel a little wild, like you're a rebellious teenager sneaking out past curfew, but trust me, once you get a taste of that sweet, guilt-free rest and relaxation, you'll be hooked.

1. Make "me time" non-negotiable. Schedule it like a doctor's appointment. You don't need a fancy trip; thirty

minutes in the tub after a week of kid drop-offs, work chaos, and life juggling can be pure magic. Turn off your phone and hit "power down" like it's your job. Yes, people will suddenly "need" you—but hold the line. Saying "no" to others means saying "yes" to you.

2. I have a self-care jar—basically my very own Magic 8 Ball for "me" time. Inside are ideas like Netflix binges, face masks, long drives, sauna sessions…you get the vibe. When it's time to recharge, I reach in and let fate decide. Make your own. Throw in anything that lights you up—take a walk, try a pottery class, or even glassblowing (because why not?). Once a week, pull something out and just do it. It's like giving your future self a little love note.
3. Get outside in nature's free therapy. Take a walk, sit in the sun, or hike a trail—even if you're just power-walking to your favorite coffee spot. Fresh air hits different when you're close to losing it.

Quittin' Time

"Don't spend time beating on a wall,
hoping to transform it into a door."

—COCO CHANEL, THE WOMAN WHO COULD LITERALLY LAUGH IN FRENCH AND MADE THE LBD EVERY WOMAN'S SECRET WEAPON

We've been brainwashed into thinking quitting = losing, but honestly? Staying in a soul-sucking situation is the real L. And don't even hit me with "What doesn't kill you makes you stronger." Nah, Nietzsche—I'm pretty sure you never had to balance a career, relationships, mental health, and trying not to eat an entire block of cheese at 2:00 a.m.

Quitting isn't failing—it's survival. Sometimes the best move you can make is to throw in the towel and walk away like a badass in a movie explosion. Life's too short to suffer through something that makes you want to scream into a pillow.

Know the difference between something worth fighting for and something that's just dragging you down. Quitting isn't weak—it's smart AF.

Hives Are Not a Good Sign

It was the beginning of 2024. I was weeks away from starting my new Hulu show, *Paradise*, and in the midst of writing this book. My genius self didn't think I was busy enough, so I signed up for a Zoom screenwriting class. I already have three kids, three dogs, a show, and a book. But whatever. This is definitely a good idea.

I went to the first class and instantly broke out in hives. The instructor presented the syllabus—hives were not on them. Instead, it was daily homework, daily check-ins from the instructor, and weekly Zoom meetings. Shit, I was going to be busier than a dog chasing two tails. What moron thought this was a good idea again?

I saw myself turning into Holden Caulfield, the delinquent of the class—not turning in assignments, not doing the homework, and leaving every two-hour Zoom about an hour and forty-five minutes early. The bottom line: I didn't want to be there. But this overachieving Capricorn did not want to quit. I was raised with the idea that quitting is for losers, so I talked myself into going back the next week.

Whaddya know? I broke out in hives again! That was when I decided to *fuggetaboudit*! I reframed everything I'd been taught: "Quitting is for *winners*!" I had to remind myself that maybe—just maybe—I wasn't a total failure for tapping out. I mean, it's not like I was sitting around binge-watching *Love Is Blind* in my underpants all day. My schedule was already a three-ring circus starring as an actress, a writer, and the unpaid chauffeur of tiny humans. If anything, quitting was proof that I respected my own limits. Maybe I could circle back to it toward the end of the year when the load would be considerably lighter.

I gave myself permission to leave. I instantly felt freer, lighter, and more in control of the things I had already committed to. The hives cleared the next day, and I was one less Zoom away from spiraling into chaos.

The Show Is Over

We were sitting at the bar, swirling our glasses of Brunello, while these thoughts swirled through my head: *OK, he hasn't seen her in four months and swore it was over. He's changed. I know he has! I can feel it. Plus, his mom told him to tell me hello. So, yeah.*

Paul #3 (all my boyfriends are named Paul, remember?) and I were celebrating a reunion dinner. We had dated for about a year when I found out he had a side chick. I called it off, and after months of him saying he could finally keep his dick in his pants, here we were. After exchanging some sweet wine-stained kisses, conversations about how he was finally ready to settle down, a lot of eye-fucking, and a branzino, we went back to his place.

Hmm, that's odd. Why is the living room light on inside the house? All the lights were off when we left. My knight in shining armor told me to wait outside while he investigated this true-crime show happening inside. I was bravely on the ready with my phone in hand to call 911 as soon as I got a whiff of the intruder. Yes, my adrenaline was pumping, but I was floating on a cloud. Paul #3 wasn't a fuck boy after all! Like a Netflix password, he wasn't going to be shared with anyone other than myself! As soon as we caught our burglar and the SWAT team took him away, we'd be on our way to bliss.

Wait...is that a woman's voice on the inside? A female burglar?! WOW! She's got balls!

Hold on, are they fighting? Why is he arguing with this criminal? Should I call 911? What's happening?

At that point, he threw open the front door, screaming, "I told you not to come over tonight," while a voice from inside followed him: "That's not what you said last night. Why can't we just talk?"

It was none other than Miss Side Chick.

Learn How to Take Your Cue

After years of rehearsing entrances and exits on stage, I knew an exit when I saw one. I didn't get angry. I didn't ask for an explanation. I didn't care to confront the understudy in this play. It was quittin' time. Time to walk away.

I calmly got in my car and drove down Sunset Boulevard toward my apartment. Paul #3 was chasing after me, screaming, "Please, let me explain," while she was chasing after him, begging, "Why her? Pick me."

Sister, there is not even a sprinkle of BS in this story. That's exactly what she said. I knew it was time to go—and I hope she got the memo, too.

You are not a failure if you decide to pack it up and pack it in on a relationship that's not good for you. It's one thing if you want to continue working on it, and you have the mental stamina, but if your nervous system is rattled by a chaos you can't calm, that's your cue. You could give it one more day or ten, but it's time to call it in. By surrendering your relationship, you save yourself.

We've been conditioned since birth to think quitting means failing. But real courage is knowing the difference between prioritizing your mental health and just being a lazy sack of bones. There's no reward at the end of your life for "toughing it out." When we arrive at the pearly gates of Heaven, God is not handing out any plaques because you "endured" through life instead of "living" it. It's important to learn when to simply walk away. Walk away and don't look back. You're not going in that direction anyway.

Turn the Mirror Back on You

Like most women, you're probably guilty of biting off more than you can chew. We are all multitasking, people-pleasing, I-can-fix-it queens. But these moments need to be assessed so you don't lose yourself. Here are some things to think on.

1. Is your relationship or job bringing you more joy or straight-up pain? Are you constantly fighting, avoiding conflict, or dreading walking into the office? If it feels like an emotional tug-of-war you're losing, it's time to check in with yourself. If you're anything like me, communicate all your needs before—say what you want, ask for what you need. But if you've done all that, and you're still stuck in Misery Town…there's your answer. Life's too short to settle for anything that drains your soul. Choose joy—or at least choose peace.
2. Why do you want to quit? Is it because it's adding more to your plate unnecessarily, or are you giving up on

yourself? If it's the second one, listen up—quitting on you is never the answer. You're stronger than you give yourself credit for. Saddle up, sister—you're about to see how awesome you are. Attack the challenge with confidence.

3. Picture yourself completely out of the situation you're thinking of leaving. How does it feel? Are you happy, relieved? Or are you filled with regret? That right there will give you your answer.

Regrets Are for Sissies

"I'd rather regret the things I've done than regret the things I haven't done."

—THE RED-HEADED TORNADO IN HEELS, LUCILLE BALL

We all have them: those little nags in the back of our minds like mosquitoes you can't quite swat away. And while some people can brush off regrets like dust on their shoulders, I've always had one main rule when it comes to taking risks. It goes something like this: Will I look back on this moment from my deathbed and regret not taking the chance? My Aries-rising self has propelled me into many situations I didn't think through. Did it always work out for me? Nope. Do I regret them? Nope.

Whether it's never chasing your dreams, sticking around in a relationship that's deader than disco, skipping time with loved ones, or biting your tongue on what matters most, don't let fear leave you with a bucket full of "coulda, woulda, shoulda." Even if you trip over your own feet, it's not a mistake if you learn something from it.

An Affair Not to Regret

When I had my little affair in college, I knew what I was doing was wrong, but I couldn't keep myself from doing it. I mean, he had the kind of smile that would make a nun rethink her vows. Like a fish on a line, I was hooked and couldn't pull away.

Being a musician, he opened me up to a world of art and music, of poetry and unfiltered, messy beauty I hadn't seen before. Until him, my life was about as exciting as watching grass grow. Like a carefully curated gallery, everything was neat, and I did exactly what was expected of me in every moment. Yawn. He was like graffiti on a blank wall. He showed me how to see beauty in the decay, in the chaos, in moments that didn't have tidy explanations.

You see, pumpkin, with Paul #2, I didn't experience love—I experienced life. He introduced me to a world beyond textbooks and routines, a world where you could sit in a room with strangers and, with the strum of his guitar, feel connected. We'd go to these underground clubs, the kind you'd never find unless you knew someone who knew someone, and there he'd be, playing his heart out while the room buzzed with energy. He introduced me to life outside of SMU and meal plans.

Yes, getting caught was worse than a kick in the teeth, and the guilt hit harder than a bad hangover, but what I gained was more than I ever lost. I found a kind of freedom I didn't know I needed. He taught me to stop overthinking every choice like it was a math problem with one correct answer. My college self had been so tied up in what I *should* do that I'd forgotten what I *wanted* to do. He taught me to lean into my impulses, to explore, to accept that sometimes life doesn't always have a clear right or wrong.

And I also learned I'll never have another affair again. I was a wuss for not admitting that I had already checked out of my relationship. But I had to go through this in order to learn these lessons. So…been there, done that, and certainly don't need to do it again, but yeah—still no regrets.

Don't Die with Your Song Still Inside You

It was 2015, and life was in the thick of being lifey. I'd sit for hours staring at a blank computer screen, knowing I had a book inside of me—something shaped by years of struggles, lessons, and hard-earned wisdom. The nudge was relentless. But I couldn't untangle my thoughts. I'd stare at the cursor like I was waiting for the words to come out.

Eight years later, in 2023, the Screen Actors Guild hit the brakes and went on strike. It was a stand-off that saw actors everywhere put their paychecks on the back burner, trading a year's worth of gigs for promises of fairer treatment across the business. With the strike dragging on and opportunities disappearing faster than a tampon at the bottom of a purse, I figured it was time to make my own luck. Remember that book I wanted to write?

Between the familiar hum of self-doubt—"I've never written a book before. What if it isn't any good? What if no one reads it?"—another voice was louder. "*But what if you don't even try?*"

So, I threw caution to the wind and started writing—one page at a time, stumbling forward like a blindfolded kid at a piñata party, no clue if I was hitting the mark or just whacking at thin air. But hey, if I crash and burn, at least I'll know I went down swinging. Eighty-five pages later, it became the proposal for this book.

However, not everyone was cheering me on. When I told my old agents I was writing a book, they laughed me out of the room. "You don't have anything to say," they chimed in. "Don't waste your time."

One especially brilliant three piece suit with a mouth said, "Wait until you're sixty-five and write a memoir. Until then, just memorize your lines—it pays better." I was floored.

But I couldn't shake the feeling that this was something I had to do, that my voice deserved a shot in the spotlight just as much as any role I'd played. I wanted to pour my experiences and face plants into something that could live outside of me, something that others could hold and even feel less alone for having read. The thought of looking back one day and knowing I let fear hold me back? That felt about as appealing as getting a root canal from Stevie Wonder. I could see it all too clearly: me on my deathbed, staring at a blank page I never had the guts to fill—finally reaching for a pen when it's too late.

Don't let your story gather dust inside you. We all have a tale worth telling—one that's about more than snack schedules and whatever mystery stain appeared on the couch. Be bold. Take a chance. And as my stepfather always said, "If you're going to invest in something, invest in yourself."

Life Doesn't Have a Rewind Button

A modern woman's calendar looks like a game of Tetris on level ninety-nine, crammed with meetings, deadlines, doctor's appointments, kids, and a couple of desperate reminders to "hydrate."

Every day is a mad dash, all while we try to convince ourselves we're "making memories" when we finally toss a PB&J to the kids on the way to soccer practice. And at the end of the day, we still say, "I just need five more minutes…" Because, hey, we like that inbox to read "zero," don't we?

But the reality is, one of the biggest regrets people carry with them as they get older is that they spent too much time chained to their desks and not enough time with the people who make life worth living.

There's a reason nobody looks back at the end of their life wishing they'd spent more time in the office—at the end of the day, it's the laughter around the dinner table, the lazy Sunday mornings, and the hugs that linger a little longer that we really remember. So, clear a little space in that Tetris board of a schedule and spend it on what truly matters. None of us are making it out of here alive, and believe me, your 401k isn't exactly a warm hug when life hits the fan. But your people? They'll be there, keeping you cozy when the world gets cold. #NoRegrets

Turn the Mirror Back on You

Life doesn't offer second chances, so make this one count. Here are some questions to help you steer clear of regret and live a life that's unapologetically you.

1. Are you speaking up about the things that bother you? Whether they're big or small, the silence can grow heavy, and if you keep swallowing your feelings, they won't disappear—they'll just make themselves at home and start taking up way too much space. What if you'd voiced that worry, shared that idea, or set that boundary? What if speaking up could save a relationship or spark a change you've been hoping for? By holding back, you miss the chance to create changes that could truly enrich your life.
2. Okay, stay with me—imagine you're already dead (I know, morbid, but stay). If you could live your life backward, what risks would you take knowing there'd be zero consequences? Would you leave that thankless relationship or soul-sucking job? Finally tell your crush you've been mentally planning your wedding since 2017? Maybe he's been doing the same. Picturing yourself at the end of the line can be weirdly clarifying.
3. Are you prioritizing the people and things that fill your cup or just checking things off a to-do list? Trust me, the next time your daughter asks you to play, even if it's 6:00 p.m., and your emails are screaming at you, say yes. It'll fill your heart in more ways than any email ever could.
4. Your dreams are supposed to make you break into a sweat. Have you been true to your dreams even if they seem "unrealistic"? Silence the naysayers and go for it. You know what they say: "If your dreams don't scare you, they're not big enough."

Rewrite Old Stories

"You wanna fly, you got to give up the shit that weighs you down."

—TONI MORRISON, THE BEYONCE OF THE LITERARY WORLD. HER BOOK BELOVED WILL REARRANGE YOUR HEART.

Listen up, buttercup! This thing here called life? It really is a game—and you get to play it however you damn well please. You create the rules. You can smash your boss's face into his birthday cake (bold move—probably leads to unemployment), or send your mother-in-law a card that reads, "Happy birthday, wench. Your son is a man-child." (That one ends in awkward Thanksgiving dinners for life.)

The choice is yours.

The point is, every action starts with a thought, and every thought shapes your outcome. If you want a different result, you've got to start with a different thought. But the majority of us have adopted beliefs that were placed upon us by others even from the time we were snot-nosed little whippersnappers. So, it's time to take a closer look at those narratives and sus out the places where you've been operating inside someone else's story.

Santa Is Real, and Other Lies Our Parents Told Us

Our parents told us a fat white man in a red suit climbs down our chimney to bring us presents his elves spent all year making. We believed them. "Don't cross your eyes, or they could get stuck that way." *We believed them.*

If my mother told me marriage meant chasing each other with a baseball bat, I'd have several assault charges against me by now. From nagging partners to disapproving parents to judgy coworkers and more, we were fed ideas, thoughts, and beliefs that didn't actually resonate with us, yet they're living rent-free in our subconscious minds.

You're no longer a child, and the insane myths are no longer gonna fly. It's time to step into your badassery and rewrite your belief system.

It took me hours of deep-diving into Dr. Joe Dispenza's teachings to realize this wild truth: We're basically walking around operating on default settings from the past—stuff we didn't even sign up for!

Remember hearing things like "Life is hard," "Money doesn't grow on trees," or "Put others first" when you were a kid? Yeah…those weren't just harmless sayings—they were mental seeds planted deep in your subconscious, sprouting into beliefs that still run the show today.

The number-one reason your life sucks ass is because you're operating from old programming you didn't even know was there. Time to hit Control + Alt + Delete on that outdated mental software. It's time for an upgrade.

Think about it: Most of us live life on autopilot, running the same boring mental playlist on repeat. Your alarm goes off and bam: "Ugh, not this shit again." Next stop? Doom-scrolling Instagram, where you instantly feel like a failure because you're not at a Hamptons garden party, clinking Aperol spritzes with friends named Blair and Thatcher in linen outfits that somehow never wrinkle.

Then you brush your teeth, mentally spiraling over your endless to-do list while half-convinced you're having a minor heart attack because your chest feels tight—but wait, maybe it's just your bra…or capitalism. Hard to say.

Sis! Give it a rest! You're burying yourself in a low-vibrational state the minute you open your eyes! But if your first thoughts are "Today's an incredible day. Everything goes exactly as it should. My genius is alarming even to myself," you start running *those* fresh new patterns in your mind and tossing the dog-shit ones to the curb.

And I get it—we're souls having this human experience, so slipping back into old habits and outdated beliefs is part of the game. But hear me out: If you start telling yourself you're amazing the *majority* of the time, your brain will actually believe it. Your confirmation bias will kick in, and you'll only start vibing with the right kinds of people and situations. Suddenly, you're not chasing the good stuff—it's magnetically drawn to you because you've convinced every cell in your body that you're worthy AF.

Basically, fake it till you cellularly make it.

Be a Bad Bitch and Stay That Way

I need you to chase down those negative stories you've been telling yourself like they're the last pair of Gucci loafers at a sample sale. Then, swap 'em out for affirmations that make you feel like the main character.

You are literally one thought away from living a completely different life. You've got the power. It's that simple—but simple doesn't mean easy. You've gotta be tougher than the cringey, self-doubt monologue playing on repeat in your head. That voice telling you you're not good enough, not smart enough, not *whatever* enough? It's a liar.

And no, I'm not saying you need to quit your job and become a travel influencer with a Bernese mountain dog named Baxter while documenting your #VanLife journey across Europe (though, iconic?). Start small. Change one thought today—then keep going.

I'll admit, I was guilty of checking Instagram the moment I woke up. I started my day with thoughts like *Why did so-and-so get that role, and not me? Did my agent push for it? Was I not good enough?*

Talk about a buzzkill. Quitting my phone addiction felt like detoxing from caffeine and bad exes combined. It took two solid weeks to stop instinctively reaching for my phone like it was my emotional support water bottle. Instead, when my alarm went off, I'd close my eyes and visualize my day—me, frolicking through life like the lead in a rom-com where nothing bad ever happens. Even if the kids were demanding breakfast like tiny dictators, I'd give myself two extra minutes to set the vibe.

Life can be a hateful little whore, and just as easily as you can tell yourself "Everything's falling apart," or "I'm not good/

smart/pretty enough," *you can* flip the script and start hyping yourself up like the star you are:

> "I'm amazing!"
>
> "Life is always working out for me!"
>
> "I attract abundance everywhere I turn!"

Same energy—better results. Try it. You might just manifest your best life between snoozes.

Sure, it might not feel natural at first, but it's really that easy! And free! Sister, this is so much better than starting your day with doomscrolling Instagram. Instead, declare to yourself how brave you are, how smart and beautiful. Give yourself a cheeky little wink in the mirror. Even if you don't quite believe it at first, it'll soon become second nature.

But Why Am I So Pretty?

One of my favorite things to do when I'm experiencing a less-than-rockstar day is to ask *why.* Our monkey brains love a good task. So, when we ask *why,* our brains feel the need to prove it to us.

> "Why am I so pretty?"
>
> "Why is everything always working out for me?"
>
> "Why am I so smart?"
>
> "Why am I living the life of my dreams?"
>
> "Why is my ass so perky?"

Sister, don't stay connected to other people's small stories of you. We hold on to shitty beliefs like they're some kind of family heirloom. But just as you eventually outgrew your parents' lie that there's a Santa, *you're not beholden to someone else's narrative.* You have the ability to live a life that's bigger than you ever dreamed. You know why I know this? Because you're *here*. You're living. Creation doesn't make a mistake. And if you're walking around like the rest of us, you have a purpose. So quit playing small, stop borrowing other people's opinions of you, and start living the big-ass life you were meant for. You're literally built for greatness. There's no excuse to keep doing life the way you were told. As Einstein said, "The measure of intelligence is the ability to change."

Turn the Mirror Back on You

I know it sounds like something out of a science-fiction movie, but you *can* rewire your brain. Here are some ways to get you started.

1. Catch your thoughts like they owe you money. Start noticing when your brain goes full-on Negative Nancy. No judgment—just catch yourself like you're snatching a rogue receipt before it blows away. Awareness is the first step to flipping the script. These are just outdated beliefs you can put right where they belong: the garbage. Your words and beliefs become your reality. Don't let the limiting ones bite you in the ass.
2. Hit the mental "Nope" button. The second you notice that downward spiral, pause. Redirect your focus like you're changing the radio station from Everything Sucks FM to Life's Pretty Great 101. You're the DJ of

your brain—play something good. Start telling yourself "the whys."

3. Feed your mind new, positive thoughts on repeat, just like installing a system update. Feeling broke? Focus on the abundance you *do* have—the love of friends, nature's beauty, or even the perfect avocado you scored at the store. Low self-confidence? Remind yourself you're magnetic, and people can't help but be drawn to your vibe.
4. Feeling stuck in failure mode? Shift your story. Instead of seeing failure as a dead end, see it as a detour. Maybe it's redirecting you to a path you never would've considered otherwise. Maybe it's teaching you a lesson you didn't know you needed. Or maybe it's just reminding you that you're human, and humans are messy, imperfect, and beautifully resilient. Every setback is just a plot twist in your success saga. Keep showing up, and soon you'll be running smoother than ever.

Sex and Desire

"The passion, the sex, the adventure.
I want it—I want it all."

—THE ONE AND ONLY BILLIE MANN, *SEX/LIFE*

I saw two butterflies fucking today. This is not the beginning of a joke. I was going for my afternoon walk (or as I like to call it, "run"), and almost stepped on what I thought was a butterfly with the largest wingspan I had ever seen. I'd stumbled upon the LeBron James of the species.

As I bent down to take a closer look at LeBron, I noticed there was another one underneath. And they were attached! Their bottoms were fully touching, and the one on top was holding onto the wings of the other with its antennae and pumping away! Was this butterfly porn or a duel between monarchs? Afraid one of them might meet their untimely demise, I grabbed a twig and tried to separate them. NOPE. The big daddy on top gripped even tighter and the little lady on the bottom was doing some gyrating motion with her bottom! Get a room, lovers, this is a family neighborhood!

Since the dawn of time, sex and desire have been primal needs for every species on the planet. But throughout history, women have been taught that the "D" word is a dirty one. No, not *dick…desire* (although, let's be real here, a dirty dick is certainly not desirable). But the suppression of female sexuality is a widespread phenomenon. In everything from art to porn to the everyday customs of cultures around the world, we see men getting serviced by women as if it's their job. ("Of course, I'll stay at home, cook, clean, take care of the babies, and politely perform fellatio before the boys come over for UFC night!") No matter how sex-positive we might be, we are conditioned to believe that sex is not about fulfilling our biological imperative but about satisfying men.

Take It Off...Take It All Off

Sister, you were put on this earth to feel all the good feels—and getting freaky is one of them. That doesn't end just because you have children, stretch marks, or an extra bit of love around your thighs.

In the wake of shooting *Sex/Life a*nd playing Billie, a switch flipped inside my head. In every other scene, I was either masturbating or having sex, so I was *forced* to accept my body and all of its flaws in front of hundreds of millions of people worldwide. I couldn't portray this voraciously sexual character while thinking, *Are my boobs down to my knees in this light?* So, I had to "act."

I pretended I was a lioness. My eyes held a hint of mischief. I carried both a fierceness and a calmness within me at the same time. The only thing that occupied my mind was my own pleasure—and I knew I'd get it. Energetically, I wanted to devour my partner because my goal was to have the greatest orgasm known to mankind.

That was Billie. Doing this over and over translated into my real-life bedroom as well. Being on a show that centered on female pleasure changed my perspective on sex. I was playing a character who was truly selfish when it came to sexual pleasure. She wasn't afraid of criticizing her husband's position or having sex with her boyfriend in the back bedroom during a party. She led with *her* pleasure in mind, and that was revolutionary. It's not common to see female characters portrayed like this.

Eventually, I started leading with my pleasure first, too. I spoke up. I instructed him to go higher, faster, or slower. Men are so good about going after their pleasure during intercourse, instructing you on what they like, and we can all stand to learn from that. Your partner will only want to please you more, so make it all about *you*!

Truly, having no more fucks to give about my body was liberating. I no longer cared about my deflated, stretch-marked boobs. Have you seen the excess skin around my stomach that I earned after my twins? That doesn't bother me anymore either. I deliberately showed my stomach in season two of *Sex/Life* to signal to women all over the world that no one is perfect, and our bodies are beautiful just the way they are. It made such a splash that *Vogue* magazine did an article about it titled "*Sex/Life* Is a Steamy Celebration of the Post-Baby Body." Women around the world wrote to me saying how freeing it made them feel to see that.

Sister, we all have flaws. We all have things we feel insecure about. But love yourself and your body regardless. Look how amazing it is. You can put it through the ringer, and it still gets you from point A to point B. From drinking until you were sideways to giving birth to babies, your body has never let you down. We should look upon our bodies as a temple, a sacred place of worship. As a matter of fact, when was the last time you held yourself and said, "Thank you"? Close your eyes and do it now. I'll wait. We all can benefit from loving our bodies more.

You Are the Sexual Revolution We All Need

While the empowerment movement has done some serious heavy lifting, we're still fighting to own our pleasure without apology. Personally, I credit *Sex/Life* for literally putting it all front and center—storylines that normalize female pleasure and actually make people think. Based on the DMs flooding my inbox after the show, women were clam-slammed more than ever with realizations about their own desires (don't everyone thank me at once).

But here's the deal, buttercup: We all need to be part of this revolution—or we'll keep getting royally screwed by a system that sexualizes us while still treating our desire like it's something shameful. Male desire? Casually celebrated. Female desire? Cue the pearl clutching. In some parts of the world, women can still face serious consequences just for expressing themselves. It's beyond overdue for us to flip the script.

You have the power to rewrite the narrative. Be vocal. Be bold. Be unapologetic. And for the love of Lady Gaga, stop slut-shaming. If another woman's got sexual confidence on lock, cheer her on and take notes.

Sex isn't some glitch in the system—it's a feature of being human. No matter how you identify, owning your desire is essential to understanding yourself and sharing your most sacred, badass parts with another person. Be your own favorite. Give shame the middle finger. And for God's sake—get yours.

Turn the Mirror Back on You

I know! It's hard to speak up about what gets you in the mood when most of the messages we've heard have been trying to get us to shut up! Here are some of my favorite tools for building confidence about our desire. Let's talk about sex, baby!

1. Your partner's probably a lot of things—but a mind reader? Not one of them. I don't care how steamy things were in the beginning—you've gotta communicate. A healthy sex life thrives on talking about what turns you on and what doesn't. When things feel loving and safe, bring it up—without making it a TED Talk on what they're doing wrong. Frame it as exploring together, not fixing something. Tell them how hot they are and how much you love being with them, then share what new things you'd like to try. Pro tip: Be as open to listening as you are to sharing. You might just discover they've got some fantasies they've been keeping under wraps too.
2. If the thought of having a serious sex talk makes you break out in hives, relax—you don't have to stage a summit at the UN. Try lightening the mood. Go out for coffee and make a list of fun, spicy things you've always wanted to try. Dirty talk with a side of sex in a semi-public place? Check. Be playful. And for the love of lattes, don't forget to laugh. Life's too short for boring convos—or boring sex.

3. Use "I" statements. Instead of "You don't touch me the way I like," try "I'd love it if you touched me like this"—and show him. Trust me, he's not gonna be defensive when he's getting a live demo from the person he's very into. Consider this "on-the-job training" he'll be thrilled to attend.

Showers

"There's no half-singing in the shower, you're either a rock star or an opera diva."

—JOSH GROBAN, THE SINGER WHO SOUNDS LIKE THE LOVE CHILD OF A CASHMERE BLANKET AND CHAMOMILE TEA.

Step away from the shampoo bottle now. Don't do it! Don't you dare pick it up. I want you to sit. Yes, that's right! Sit down and just take a few minutes for yourself. Feel the stream of the water hit your eyes and your head, and trickle down the back of your neck, and just exist. Who cares if the nanny stays late or your partner has to mine the potatoes out of the oven? This is your time. You've spent all day being the CEO of Chaos, Inc.—now, surrender under the spray and just be.

The shower isn't just where you rinse off—it's where you release. The kids' demands, your boss's passive-aggressive emails, your mom's unsolicited parenting tips—let them spiral down the drain. No need for a yoga mat, a sage bundle, or a fancy retreat in Bali—this is your sanctuary. The only fee? Hot water and five uninterrupted minutes.

I learned this during one epically disastrous Christmas in 2019. The kids were sick, my marriage was on the rocks, and holiday cheer was out of stock. So, while the chaotic little cherubs finally napped, I stole twenty minutes and did the only thing I could think of that didn't require words, answers, or holding anyone else together—I stepped into the shower. Just me, the water, and a fragile grip on sanity.

I turned on the water and…dropped. My knees hit the floor like my soul had given out. And then the tears came—chest-heaving, snot-dripping, ugly-crying. I was sobbing like I was getting paid by the tear. I started praying—or maybe begging. "Dear God, Jesus, whoever's up there—*please.* I'm exhausted, I'm lost, and I'm done pretending I have it all figured out. I thought life was supposed to be more than just surviving. I feel like I'm living in a cage. Show me that there's still some kind of purpose here, that I'm not invisible. If you're listening… throw me a bone. Anything."

Did I win the lotto? No. Did angel choirs start singing? No. Any lightning bolt epiphanies? Also no. But something shifted. I felt…lighter. Like someone had cracked a window in a room that had been suffocating. I felt heard. Not fixed—but witnessed. And somehow, that was enough. A few weeks later, I booked *Sex/Life*, and the rest is history. Coincidence? I think not.

Since that day, the shower has become my holy ground. Even when I only have five minutes, I sit on the floor and let the water wash away the noise. No deadlines, no guilt, no interruptions—just me, my thoughts, and the universe taking notes.

Moral of the story? Surrender beneath the spray. Someone's listening—even if you're butt-naked, sobbing on tile, and running out of conditioner.

Turn the Mirror Back on You

Carve out shower time as sacred time, sister! And if showers ain't your thing, get creative. Pick a secluded park bench, a hole-in-the-wall cafe frequented by only you, or anywhere else you can surrender and reconnect to yourself.

1. Stop treating your shower like a pit stop at a car wash. Let that space be your meditation den. A lot of times, I shower with the lights off and nothing but a few flickering candles for company.
2. As the water rushes down the drain, pretend it's taking all your worries with it—bad moods, annoying group texts, your boss's weird tone, and that one cringe thing you said three years ago. Let the water lighten your load.
3. Close your eyes and repeat some of these particularly affirmy affirmations:
   - I'm in the flow of life—like, VIP access, front row, no waiting.
   - The path forward is lighting up like a neon runway at Fashion Week.

- I'm done carrying this heavy-ass burden. Universe, it's yours now—handle it.
- The right solution's already in motion. I'm ready to receive.

This Too Shall Pass

"Life is amazing. And then it's awful. And then it's amazing again. And in between the amazing and the awful, it's ordinary and mundane and routine. Breathe in the amazing, hold on through the awful, and relax and exhale during the ordinary. That's just living heartbreaking, soul-healing, amazing, awful, ordinary life. And it's breathtakingly beautiful."

—L. R. KNOST, SUPERHUMAN MOM TO SIX AND THE GURU OF GENTLE PARENTING, QUOTED EVERYWHERE FROM HOLLYWOOD TO PARLIAMENT

Tom Hanks was my first crush. Weird intro to this chapter, I know, but keep reading. I remember being, like, zero years old, watching *Bosom Buddies*, when I turned into a little coochie kitten for this big-nosed, curly-haired, skinny man. I was smitten. The more crushable male paramours of the time were men like Rob Lowe, Richard

Gere, David Bowie, Steven Tyler, and a slew of other famous men wearing acid-washed jeans and a tub of hair gel. Yet my attention belonged to America's future history professor. The infatuation developed through *Splash* and kept growing until *Charlie Wilson's War*. After that, the crush fizzled out, and now I just want to gift him a cozy sweater and spend Thanksgiving with him and Rita. Something tells me he roasts a mean turkey, and Rita's sides would steal the show.

Having that invisible seat at Thanksgiving means I run to every Tom Hanks movie and devour every interview like its comfort food. I recently watched one where he spoke about not getting too attached to the critiques of a film, whether it's good or bad. "This too shall pass," he said, adding that the phrase is true not just for the unfavorable reviews but for the flattering ones as well. Daddy, ahem, I mean Tom, explained that he used to get crushed by the negative reviews and then would be soaring like an eagle for the positive ones. That kind of emotional mindfuck is exhausting, so now, he's adopted a more grounded outlook towards them. Everything is but a moment in time and carries whatever energetic weight he assigns to it. "This too shall pass" applies to all of them regardless of where the critiques land. It isn't just a phrase—it's a permission slip to exhale, detach, and keep your feet on the ground no matter which way the wind blows.

When *Sex/Life* dropped, the reviews were a wild ride. One critic would call the show "a revolutionary battle cry," while another basically said it had more plot holes than Swiss cheese. I was either flying high or face down in the dirt.

So, I decided to channel my inner Tom and adopt "This too shall pass." A great review? Loved it! But did it need to be broadcast from the International Space Station while the military saluted me from Earth with a flyover? Not anymore. It didn't define me. I'd smile, soak in the warm fuzzies like a cozy bath, and move the hell on.

A bad review? Same vibe. When someone called Billie Mann the "horniest, most one-dimensional character" in TV history, I actually laughed out loud. Like, fair play, my guy. But I didn't clutch my pearls or spiral into existential dread. I let it roll off, because—say it with me—*this too shall pass*. And it did. Just like bad perms, Y2K panic, and those terrifying low-rise jeans from the early 2000s. Time keeps it moving, and thank God for that.

Though this mindset started with my work, it spilled right into my personal life, fast and loud—because if I wasn't going to let career highs and lows define me, why would I hand over that power to relationship drama, parenting chaos, or any other lifey meltdown? If the universe was kicking me in the tits? You bet this too shall pass. And if life was making out with me tongue-first, whispering sweet nothings into my ear? Same deal. It's all temporary. Everything only had the weight I assigned to it.

Life isn't about winning every round or avoiding the lows—it's about showing up through it all. Laugh, cry, dance, scream, create, fight, whatever. You're here for the whole-ass ride. Live in the flow. As the only man who could punch you and inspire you at the same time, Bruce Lee said, "You put water into a bottle, it becomes the bottle. You put it in a teapot, it becomes the teapot. Water can flow, or it can crash. Be water, my friend."

Be shapeless. Be grounded. Be water. Because water knows: This too shall pass.

Turn the Mirror Back on You

If you're having trouble surrendering to the ebbs and flows of life, here are some things that can help.

1. Accept that you can't control everything in life. Sure, you can plan your day until it's as smooth as butter, but things can still go haywire. The one thing you can control is your attitude. Nothing lasts forever, so be mindful of how you show up.
2. Feeling pissed off, sad, or angry? Give it time. Feeling happy, understood, or like you've got life totally figured out? Give it time. Spoiler alert: Everything changes. When you realize that life moves in cycles and seasons, you stop being a victim of circumstance. You can enjoy the highs without clinging to them—and survive the lows without thinking they'll last forever. Stay open. Accept the ebb and flow. Life's gonna kick dirt in your face now and then—but it'll also hand you flowers. Just keep moving through it all.
3. Be in the now. Stop romanticizing the past and catastrophizing the future. Look for something positive in the present. Some days you may have to look harder than others, but beauty is always all around.
4. Remind yourself that better days are sure to come. You know how I know this? Because they always have.

Trust

"You never know how strong you are until being strong is your only choice."

—BOB MARLEY, YOU KNOW WHO HE IS

Take a seat, sis—this one is intense.

My father, God bless his soul, was a drug addict. He was abusive not only to my mother, but one fateful summer afternoon, to me, too. He was in the middle of a bad episode when he took me outside, held me on his hip, and held a gun to my head.

I was six and don't remember anything prior to this moment. But I remember what happened after.

I remember how cold the metal was against my temple. I remember the way he held me, his head hung low, too heavy to lift, as silent tears ran down his face. Over and over he whispered that I was too good, too pure, to be living in this world, and it was time for us to "go home."

His drug-fueled plan was clear: kill me then himself. In his twisted mind, my mother would follow, taking her own life in despair. That afternoon, as she returned home from work, she called out to us. No answer. Silence. Then, the sound of his gut-wrenching sobs pulled her outside, like a siren. She froze. Her breath caught in her throat.

You know those scenes in movies where one person catches someone else cheating, or there's a car crash, and suddenly time slows to a crawl, each second stretching out until everything freezes? That's exactly what it felt like. I saw my mother's face collapse, dropping six feet below ground when she saw me in my dad's arms. I could hear her heartbeat, a slow echoing thud. It was as if the air had thickened, every small detail magnified in perfect, painful clarity. And there we were, in that split-second moment, frozen in time.

She moved toward him quietly, with a gentleness as if she were approaching a wounded animal, fragile and sacred. I don't remember her exact words, only the murmur of her voice. She reached for the gun, her hand open and waiting, and he surrendered it to her, the metal slipping into her palm as he crumbled, collapsing onto her shoulder.

Then, without a word, she wrapped her arm around me and ushered me inside. As we moved away, I caught one last glimpse of my father, crying on the ground, surrounded by a small puddle that seemed to hold all the heaviness in the world.

Alongside my superhero of a mother, my own innocent naiveté shielded me. At such a tender age, I couldn't fully grasp the gravity of what was unfolding, but for reasons I still can't explain, fear never took hold of me. My attention was drawn to *him*— a certain desperation in his eyes, something so raw that in my six-year-old heart, all I could do was feel for him, and in that strange, innocent way, I felt empathy.

As the years passed, it came as no surprise that my relationship with my father was never simple. Life with an addict is like living on the edge of a cliff—you're always waiting for a shift in the wind. My mother and I drifted through long seasons of uncertainty, each one more unpredictable than the last. When he was up, it felt like we were touching the sky; his joy was contagious. But when he spiraled down, we plummeted with him, falling to depths so low we felt the darkness press against our chests.

Wanting to create a sense of stability, we found a temporary home between the walls of a Dallas women's shelter, our "vacation home," as my mom would sometimes joke, turning our escapes into little adventures. We'd roll in, Mom in her "we've got this" mode, ready to make new friends, convincing me we were just having another "sleepover."

My mother held me together through it all, making even the chaos feel like part of the plan. This cycle spun on for years: She'd get pulled back into his orbit by his teary apologies and promises of a fresh start. A couple years later, my mom welcomed my baby sister, Samantha, into the world, and with a newborn in her arms, life became even more challenging. This time, though, my dad was the one who left.

He would disappear for months, sometimes years at a time, popping back into our lives whenever the mood struck him. And when he did, it was a scene: We'd hear the faint strains of Willie Nelson's "Always on My Mind" rolling down the street, and there he'd be, parked in our driveway. For my sister and me, this became the signal. *Dad's back*, we'd think, sighing and grabbing our shoes. Guess it's time for a driveway reunion.

We'd find him sitting there with a mix of melancholic swagger and lingering cologne that hadn't changed since the '80s. He was always a little foggy-eyed, a little sad, like a character from a country song who didn't quite get the happy ending. He'd sit there, always under some kind of influence, quiet, asking us how we were. And the rest of the hour, we sat in silence, listening to Willie on repeat. It was as if the lyrics were speaking things he didn't know how to say. If it wasn't so depressing, it would've been ridiculous—but it was both.

And so it went: a revolving door of under-the-influence returns and mysterious disappearances. We'd roll our eyes and joke about the next installment of *Dad Returns*, half expecting Willie Nelson to pull into the driveway himself one day. Life with my dad was a roller coaster that had us holding on tight, if only to keep our balance.

As my sister grew older, the veil began to lift, and she started to see the troubled man our father truly was. The warmth she'd once held for him cooled bit by bit as the pieces of his story fell into place. My own relationship with him had long been reduced to distant exchanges. Finally, for her own peace, my sister made the difficult choice to step away, realizing that some doors, once closed, are better left that way.

But our father, unwilling to face his own demons, pointed the finger at me. He became convinced that I was the reason she had distanced herself, that I had somehow robbed him of his baby girl. He was angry and began leaving me messages with words that cut deeper than I was prepared for. His voice was a mixture of desperation and rage, warning me that the next time he saw me, he'd bury me six feet under for turning Samantha against him. It was a haunting echo of his earlier threats, of him once holding a gun to my head. That dark tale of ending my life—a story he clung to—was too much to bear. I changed my number and never spoke to him again. I was twenty-two.

He died when I was thirty-five. Alone. Overdose. I cried for months, not mourning his death but the loss of the hope that things would ever change.

Chin Up, Buttercup

Hello! Paging Dr. Freud! Can someone say *daddy issues*?!

Let's lighten it up a bit, shall we! Look, I've hit some of life's lowest notes, feeling like each day was just another layer of heavy. This book is built on me kissing rock bottom. But this experience with my father, and every other that was vomited onto my lap, taught me that I will pull myself back up no matter how steep the climb. I've learned that I can live in a women's shelter and make it out and fly. I've learned that I can leave a union of nearly twenty years with three kids and soar. It is amazing what I was capable of surviving when I didn't have a choice. Now, when I'm dealt a shitty card, I've played enough rounds to know I'm not going to fold.

Trust is a muscle; the more you use it, the stronger it becomes. And over the years, it has lifted me up when my own strength felt lacking, reminding me that even on my weakest days, the upward swing is coming. Why? Because it always, always does.

Here are some nuggets of wisdom I've gathered along the way.

1. Whether you have good days or bad, the bad will see the light. You may not be able to see it at first, but it will. It always does.
2. When you fall, get back up. The view is better up there anyway.

3. Just because life is a pain doesn't mean you have to be one.
4. When one door closes, let it. It's not the end of the world. It just means it's time to open a new one.
5. The resistance to chocolate is futile. Always.
6. A lazy Sunday is good for everyone.
7. Don't focus too much on being a "nice" person. Focus more on being an honest one. It's what will ultimately serve the greatest good for all.
8. Hurt people hurt people. When you heal yourself, you heal everyone around you.
9. Want to communicate with your soul? Look in the mirror and tell yourself, "I love you." You are speaking with an energy that goes far beyond your eyes.
10. Geek out over the things that make you happy. Life's too short not to.
11. Just because you're good for someone doesn't mean they're good for you. Learn the difference.
12. It's OK to get angry with God. He can take it.
13. It's OK to let your children see you cry.
14. I'd rather be a fool for love, put myself out there and lose, than be "too cool for school" and never even try.
15. Life is not about being "right." It's about having fun.
16. Prioritize your peace.
17. When you think of something nice about someone, tell them.
18. *While You Were Sleeping* is a Christmas movie you can watch year-round.
19. An old dog can learn new tricks.
20. It's never too late to be happy.

Yes, life can be hard, but you don't have to be. Don't sweat the big or small stuff, because in the end, everything is small. Your job is to let go and have fun. No matter what curveballs life has thrown, I've been the one to catch them, dust myself off, and keep going. Trust the universe, and more importantly, trust yourself. *You will never let yourself down.* Winston Churchill said it best: "If it feels like hell, keep walking." Trust. God never puts the stars in the wrong place.

Turn the Mirror Back on You

It's hard to imagine life can be anything other than a hairy bag of dicks when you're swimming knee-deep in them, but ask yourself the following in order to prove that good days are around the corner.

1. Has the universe ever totally ghosted you before? Sure, it's sent some mixed signals (looking at you, 2020), but somehow, you're still here—alive and growing. Think back to your most epic meltdown—the one where you were convinced life was over (probably involving a breakup, a job rejection, or a horrifying haircut). You survived. You moved on. Seasons change and so do you.
2. What's the worst that can happen? Let's be real—worrying hasn't exactly fast-tracked your dreams, has it? Trusting the universe isn't blind optimism; it's about knowing that you'll handle whatever comes. You might not get exactly what you want, but you'll get what you need—and often, something even better. Think of the universe like Amazon Prime—sometimes delayed, but it always delivers.

3. When life feels stuck, help someone else. Get out of your head. Serving others shifts your perspective and reminds you you're part of something bigger. Volunteer at your kids' school, your community, or even a children's hospital. Nothing puts things in perspective more than spending time with a child struggling to be well.
4. Look for little signs. Sometimes God's messages aren't skywriting or burning bushes—they're small moments: a kind text, a sunset, a parking spot when you needed one. Proof you're not forgotten.

Unapologetically Unbothered

"Don't let anyone dim your light because it's shining in their eyes."

—SOMEONE SO COSMICALLY MYSTERIOUS, THEY GO BY... "UNKNOWN"

Alright, ladies, gather round because we're about to dive deep into the golden rule of life: Never, and I mean never, play small for anyone. Not for your boss, your parents, your partner, your BFF, or that coworker who thinks you're "a bit much." If someone is intimidated by the giant neon light you carry that radiates from the inside out, well, they can suck it. You are not here to dumb yourself down to make someone else feel more comfortable. So, be unapologetic in your magic. The right people will bask in your light. And the ones that don't? Sayonara, sucker.

Dumped in Aisle Five

In my early twenties, I dated a guy who worked in finance. Now, I'm the kind of bitch who double-dips at parties, so I don't know what I was thinking. We're in the cereal aisle at Albertsons, all romantic, holding hands and stealing kisses between boxes of Lucky Charms and Cinnamon Toast Crunch. Then, it happens: Phil Collins's "In the Air Tonight" starts playing over the speakers. And if you know, you know…the drum solo. It's not just music; it's a full-on spiritual experience. So, naturally, I'm belting the lyrics and air-drumming my heart out, totally lost in my joy.

Cue Mr. Finance—he yanks his hand away, turns bright red, and hisses, "Why are you so desperate for attention? Stop being such a stage whore!"

Whoa, buddy. Pump the brakes. Will Frosted Flakes calm you down? It's Phil Collins and the famed drum solo, idiot. Everyone with a heartbeat knows toe-taps won't cut it; *you have to air-drum this moment.* He said I was being obnoxious and unladylike, and between this and my laugh, he was secretly mortified to be seen with me.

Dear reader, I must interrupt the story to say anyone who knows me knows my laugh sounds nothing like a faint giggle. It's more like an air horn that can alert ships on the other side of the ocean.

He walked away, glancing over his left shoulder dramatically, like he was doing an ad for The CW, and said, "You're too much. You need to learn to settle down." He left me right there, in the middle of aisle five, and I never heard from him again. But the worst part? I believed him. Maybe I did need to tone it down, laugh quieter, not enjoy the drum solo so much. I wanted to shrink for him. I was willing to turn down the volume on "me" and become a watered-down version of myself—all for Mr. Cardboard Box, who had major small-dick energy.

Honey, I Shrunk Myself

We've all felt it: that nudge to tone it down, shrink a little, maybe not be so…extra. But here's the deal, sister—playing small to make others feel comfortable? That's not living; that's surviving.

Let's talk about what happens when you don't choose yourself. You start with the little compromises that you barely even notice—skipping that joke, taming your loud laugh, or "toning down" your bold ideas. It's like tiptoeing through life in shoes that are two sizes too small. And for what? People who want you to fit their mold? Newsflash: *The ones worth having in your life are the ones who'll break that mold just to make space for you.*

Imagine getting to the end of your life and thinking, "Wow, I really wish I'd played it small." No! Not one person has ever said that. Instead, the regrets come from the chances they didn't take, the times they dimmed their sparkle, the moments they didn't say, "Screw it, this is me." The only person who should be running the show in your life is you, so embrace every big, bold, extra thing about yourself.

The next time you feel the urge to downplay your personality, I want you to stop and ask yourself: "Who am I doing this for?" Because if the answer isn't "me," then know you're about to step on your own toes. Dance when there's no music, wear the brash outfit, have "unrealistic" dreams if that's who you are! Because when you live life as your full self, unapologetically, you give everyone around you permission to do the same. And that, my friend, is the ultimate gift.

Turn the Mirror Back on You

Life's way too short to be the incredible shrinking woman, so if you find yourself playing small, here are some questions to snap you back to that fabulous unapologetic energy that's all yours.

1. Are you tucking away your quirks like they're dirty laundry, just so someone else doesn't have to deal? Are you quieting yourself in moments where you normally wouldn't, whether it's with your literal voice, or even down to the way you dress? If they can't handle your extra, that's their fault. Hand them a pair of shades and shine brighter.
2. Channel your inner BFF for a second. Would she be hyping you up for living your best life, or serving you three snaps and a side-eye for putting yourself on mute? Hint: She's probably rooting for full-volume you.
3. Imagine there's zero judgment: What would you wear, say, or do? If the answer includes jazz hands, singing in public, or admitting your reality TV obsession, maybe it's time to go for it. Life's too short to pretend you don't love *Love Island*.
4. Be honest: Are you holding back because you're stressed about other people's opinions? Imagine if Beyoncé worried about what Karen from HR thought. Would we even have *Lemonade*? Exactly! Let's do a little time travel here. Picture yourself a year from now. Are you actually happy with how you're showing up in your own life? Or are you out here hiding parts of yourself just to keep everybody else comfy? You're tiptoeing around, holding back your thoughts, stuffing down your feelings—for what?! So you don't "rock the boat"? The only person

you're hurting is yourself! The ones who are meant to stay will, and for the rest: Don't let the door hit ya where the good Lord split ya.

Universe—Take a Whack at It

"The cosmos is within us. We are made of star-stuff. We are a way for the universe to know itself."

—CARL SAGAN: AN ASTRONOMER AND SCIENTIST WHO WAS WAY COOLER THAN YOU OR ME

Ahhh, the universe. The Divine. Source Energy. God. The Big Ol' Star Factory. The Head Honcho. The Cosmic Kemosabe. There are a million ways to address that magical energy that flows through each and every one of us, that singular current that connects us to every living thing on this planet from the trees to the stars. My most preferred monikers are universe and God. Every once in a while, "Hey, shithead" gets thrown in there when I'm upset, but that's only because I know God has a sense of humor.

"Are You There, God? It's Me, Sarah..."

Stephanie Money was my best friend in fifth grade—long fiery-red hair, the cutest constellation of freckles, lean muscular legs, and a volleyball player's tush. I had a unibrow. We came up with aliases—Ariel and Pocahontas—so we could pass notes about boys without getting caught in class. We thought we were master spies. But since she was the only redhead in school and I was literally always next to her, we weren't exactly criminal masterminds. Nice try, us.

One afternoon, we were walking home from school, backpacks bouncing, probably arguing about which Spice Girl we'd be that week, when I told her my brother had joined the army and was going to be shipped off to Iraq for the Persian Gulf War. Even though his favorite hobby was slapping me on the forehead and calling me "Peck," I was worried. Stephanie nodded like a wise sage and said, "If you want him to be safe, you should pray to God." No hesitation—like she was God's personal assistant and could pencil me in. Solid advice, honestly.

"Well, how do I do that?"

"Just talk to Him."

"Like, out loud? Does He know me? Can He hear me?"

"Oh, Pocahontas! You're so funny. Of course God can hear you! He knows we're talking about Him right now! Just try it tonight before you go to bed."

"Hello? God? Um…my name is Sarah. Is God your first name, or…? Is this a good time, because I can come back.… Well, if you're not too busy, I'd like to talk to you about my brother. My mom cries for him every night. Please let him be safe. Please let him come back in one piece. If you bring him back, I'll let him call me Peck for the rest of my life. I hope you hear this. Oh, can I have Sean Mayor? Sixth grader, tall…never mind, just focus on my brother please. Aaaah—men?"

Eight months later, my brother came back. In one piece. Slapping me right on the forehead and calling me Peck. Right then and there, my belief in God was born. I believed in something I could not see. That same energy that created the stars, created me, and brought my brother home. And the icing on the cake? Since I am the product of this energy, I don't have to go far to find it. I only have to look within.

It's All Connected

That energy? It's not just in answered prayers or dramatic moments. It's in everything. God, the Divine, Source—whatever you want to call it—communicates through energy, also known as vibes. Every thought you have? Vibes. Every emotion? Vibes. That gut feeling telling you not to text your ex at 2:00 a.m.? Major vibes.

It's always tuned in. Always watching. Always picking up what you're putting down. And this isn't about being perfect or high-vibe twenty-four seven. It's about trusting that there's something bigger—something unseen but eternally present—working with you, not against you. Guiding you, nudging you, rearranging things behind the scenes. Your only job is to keep your frequency honest and aligned with the life you actually want. Because trust me—*the universe is always listening.*

And when I catch myself doubting, I go back to that night in fifth grade. A scared little girl, whispering into the unknown, hoping something was on the other end.

And something was. It answered—not with words, but with a miracle wrapped in a forehead slap and the nickname "Peck."

So believe in that sparkly mystery in the sky that keeps you from texting your ex and having a full meltdown in Trader Joe's. Could it all be made up? Sure. But so is most of capitalism, and we still show up for seventeen-dollar smoothies and fifty-dollar water bottles that leak. So if you've ever made a wish at 11:11, held onto a gut feeling you couldn't explain—why not believe something bigger is guiding the rest?

God. Why not.

Turn the Mirror Back on You

If you're lacking some spiritual dimension in your life, here are some nuggets of cosmic wisdom to chew on.

1. Look at everything you've been through, everything you've survived, to get you to where you are right now, reading this book. This is exactly where you should be. Divine timing is a real thing. The master appears when the student is ready.
2. Stop trying to outsmart life like it's some impossible escape room. Surrendering your mind means releasing the mental hamster wheel and trusting the universe's GPS. When you let go of the need to control every little detail, you quiet that chaotic monkey mind. That's when your intuition

comes through loud and clear, guiding you toward your next right move.

3. Next time you're driving solo, skip the true-crime podcast and have a heart-to-heart with the universe. Speak out loud like you're at the world's most magical drive-thru: "I'll take health, love, money, and success, please. Extra abundance on the side." Stay open, and watch the universe start dropping little "Your order's being prepared" signs along the way.

Value

"You don't find your worth in a man. You find your worth within yourself and then find a man who's worthy of you."

—BEYONCE, ENOUGH SAID

I don't care how down in the dumps you feel right now—when you finally recognize your worth, you'll stop negotiating it like it's a flea market special. Ask yourself: Are you worth the cheating partner? The toxic boss? The narcissistic ex or the condescending mother-in-law? NO.

As Melanie Griffith told Alec Baldwin in *Working Girl* (iconic), "I am not steak. You can't just order me." Same goes for you. When you know your value, you won't settle for being anyone's plan B, emotional punching bag, or last-minute thought.

Now, this isn't about becoming a self-obsessed monster who throws oatmeal at their assistant because it's made with almond milk instead of water. This is about building a deep, unshakeable belief in your self-worth. You deserve the best—no disclaimers, no apologies, no fine print. Believing in yourself isn't a side hustle—it's a full-time job, and calling in sick isn't an option.

You and Gisele Had the Same Confidence...When You Were Three

Remember how you were as a child? You would cut a cunt on the playground if they took your toy. Bitch, this is my sandbox! When we're young, we have no doubt about our self-worth and what we deserve. But then, life happens. We get knocked down. We love ourselves less. We believe them when they tell us we can't do it or that we're not good enough.

Blame it on our long-lost evolutionary cousin, Caveman Carl. His brain was *wired* to focus on *danger*—like lurking saber-toothed tigers—*instead* of compliments like, "Carl you look dashing in your loin cloth today." That negativity bias helped him survive, but now it just means you're more likely to obsess over one bad comment than ten glowing compliments. Annoying, right? But here's the deal: You're not dodging predators anymore—you're dodging limiting beliefs. You've always been that badass kid in the sandbox who knew exactly what they deserved. It's time to kick Caveman Carl to the curb and reclaim your throne.

Do you recognize how great you are? You're at the top of the food chain! You create life! And, you have a killer ass. Yes, you do. (You can buy a great ass on Amazon for twenty bucks. Look up "ass pads" and thank me later. Just don't let anyone see you put them on.) As the OG of all first ladies, Eleanor Roosevelt, famously said, "No one can make you feel inferior without your consent." *Refuse to consent to making yourself feel inferior.*

You're Gonna Have to Leave Some Suckers Behind

Standing in your standards will quickly determine who's your bitch and who's not. But sister, be prepared—because it may mean leaving some ride or dies behind. The fear of abandoning people is the number-one reason we stay in situations that are beneath us. But time is precious. Don't waste it holding on to people who don't see you the way you see yourself.

Early on in my career, I had a boyfriend who was a bit more established than me say, "You're not that good, you're not that smart, and it's my job to bring you down." A real romantic, eh? That same Prince Charming also congratulated me after I won an acting award by saying, "What? You think you're good just because you can cry on cue? Guess again!" WOW. OK, Casanova. How do you say "dry" in Español? Because that's what I am now. Yes, this love story ended very quickly after that. Shocking, I know.

When you show people your worth, you'll also see who agrees. And if people don't align with how you value yourself, don't chase. Don't try to convince them. Let them go. The ones who are meant to stay will. There are people out there who would go to the ends of the earth for you. They'll take the longer route home just to stop by and give you a hug. So, accept it. And when you believe in your worth, you'll find the people who feel the same way.

Speak Up, Sis!

You can't rewrite your life if you're stuck on mute. So, speak up! If something isn't working, say it loud and clear. No high-value woman ever stayed silent while building her dream life. *What you're not changing, you're choosing.*

When you finally decide you're worthy of the life you want—and you're brave enough to say it out loud—everything shifts. You'll attract people who hype you up, not energy vampires who dim your light. It all comes down to this: knowing, deep in your bones, that you deserve the life you desire. Your worth isn't up for debate—it's yours to claim.

Turn the Mirror Back on You

If you struggle with determining your value, here are some things that can help you sync up with how absolutely amazing you are.

1. Audit your inner circle. Your tribe is your vibe. Energy drainers? Unfollow. Mood boosters? Keep 'em close. You're too valuable for half-hearted cheerleaders.
2. Why do we act like compliments are hot potatoes we can't wait to toss away? Someone tells you, "You look gorgeous!" and you're like, "No, I don't. My face is puffy." What are you doing?! This isn't a courtroom—you don't have to build a defense case against your own fabulousness. Take the win!
3. Brag like no one's watching. Start a brag book—write down every win, even the tiny ones. Seeing your greatness on paper hits different.
4. Where did those "you're not worthy" messages even come from? A parent? An ex? Society's weird rulebook? Hand that baggage right back where it came from. You're here on this planet, which means you're automatically entitled to joy, love, and all the good stuff. No permission slip needed.

Villains

"Every villain is a hero in their own mind."

—TOM HIDDLESTON, A.K.A. LOKI

What's a happy ending without its share of assholes? A lot of things are avoidable: cage diving with sharks, bangs, hand gliding. Assholes, however, are not. Although at one point you would have rather gouged your eyes out with a spoon than look at them again, you have the power to look at it differently now. We've all had someone who made our lives a living nightmare, the Regina George to your Cady Heron, the Darth Vader to your Luke Skywalker, the ex who stole your heart and your favorite hoodie. Flip your perspective to see them as your greatest teacher.

"Wait, what? Hard pass." Trust me, I get it. But these so-called villains can teach us some of the most powerful lessons. Maybe it's that boss who sends passive-aggressive emails at 2:00 a.m., or that friend who betrayed your trust by spilling your deepest secrets faster than TMZ. Maybe it's your ex who ghosted you and then had the audacity to like your Instagram selfie six months later. I know, it's giving "How dare they?" vibes. But here's where it gets interesting: What if we stopped labeling them as villains and started thinking of them as professors in the School of Life?

First, picture your villain in all their infuriating glory. Go ahead, visualize them. Are they smirking? Rolling their eyes? Maybe twirling a mustache like a Disney bad guy? Got the image in your head? Good. Now, let's reframe.

Haters Are Our Professors

I had a friend who treated her wallet like a mythical creature—always missing when the check came. She always had an excuse: left it in the car, lost it in her Gucci tote, or suddenly had to "Venmo you later" (she never did). At first, I laughed it off—girls supporting girls, right? But over time, it became clear: She didn't forget her wallet. She forgot her integrity.

What did she teach me? Stop picking up the tab for people who never bring anything to the table but appetite and excuses. A friendship isn't a charity.

A boss on set once told me to "know my place" and "not question his authority" after I questioned the meaning of a line in the script. What he really meant was "stay small so I feel big."

What did he teach me? Shrink for no one. When someone feels threatened by your power, that's not your cue to dim it—it's your cue to stand taller. Let your ambition be louder than their insecurity. Guess what? I do know my place—*at the top.*

And how about the family members who only liked me when my bank account was doing the most? They loved me when I was picking up dinner or booking vacations, but disappeared faster than a tax refund when I was the one in need.

What did they teach me? Love that's only available when you're performing or producing isn't love—it's a transaction.

Turns out, my villains were actually life coaches in disguise. Every backhanded comment, shady betrayal, and disappearing act taught me the fine art of setting boundaries. They were the pop quizzes I hadn't studied for but aced eventually. America's favorite cowboy-therapist, Dr. Phil, said it best: "You teach people how to treat you." Turns out, my "villains" were running an intensive seminar on How to Stand Up for Yourself 101.

Ex-bosses, ex-lovers, flaky former friends—they all reflected what you were willing to accept back then…and what you definitely won't tolerate now. Triggers are teachers. If someone can't see your value, that's a "them" problem, not a "you" problem. You're Elle Woods, baby, and they're the Warner who wasn't worth it.

Empathy 101

Now, I know this one's a tough pill to swallow, but sometimes your villain is hurting, too. Hurt people hurt people. Maybe that mean girl from high school was dealing with her own insecurities. Maybe your grumpy neighbor is lonely. When we practice empathy, we start to see that everyone's fighting battles we know nothing about. And listen, I'm not saying you have to send them holiday cards, but understanding their humanity can soften the edges of your anger. It's like that line from *Mean Girls*: "Calling someone ugly won't make you any prettier." Maybe your villain's been projecting their own pain, and now you can move on knowing it wasn't all about you.

Resilience 101

I know, nobody wants to think of their life's biggest jerk as some kind of wise Jedi Master. But would Cinderella have ever met Prince Charming if her stepmother hadn't been a walking HR complaint? Would Snow White have known the power of true love's kiss if she hadn't bitten that toxic apple and taken a literal dirt nap? Sometimes the universe sends you a villain not to ruin your life but to launch it.

These soul-crushing moments are when you find out what you're really made of—thunder in your belly, heart wide open, ready for the comeback of the century. Villains kick our butts into gear, sparking epic glow-ups and sweet, sweet revenge success stories. They teach us what's a "Hell yes!" and what's a "Fuck no."

Maybe you were raised by a wicked stepmother or dated someone who made the devil look like an angel. Whatever the case, these human plot twists force us to level up. They force you to find your voice, claim your power, and rewrite your story like the hero you were born to be. *Everyone in your life has a purpose—you just have to figure out what lesson they came to teach. And when you do? You win.*

Turn the Mirror Back on You

Ok, sister. You've definitely faced a few Ursula-types who tried to snatch your voice and steal your shine. Joke's on them—they were really just unpaid life coaches. Flip the script: Their chaos wasn't your downfall. It was your origin story.

1. Your villains aren't obstacles—they're messy side characters making your comeback story way more binge-worthy.

Adjust your crown and thank them for the free plot development. You're the star—they're just background chaos.

2. Grab your journal and list all the ways life's curveballs leveled you up. That shady coworker? Made you sharper than a power blazer. That dismissive ex? Taught you exactly what you don't want. Turn every plot twist into fuel for your ultimate glow-up story. This isn't a pity party—it's your self-love manifesto in the making.

Why Wait?

"Don't wait. The time will never be just right."

—NAPOLEON HILL, AUTHOR OF THINK AND GROW RICH WHICH HAS SOLD OVER 100 MILLION COPIES SINCE THE 1930S AND STILL SLAPS

Pumpkin, let me ask you a question. Do you know for a fact you're going to be walking around on God's green earth a week from today? No! No one does! So do things that make you happy *now.*

My birthday is January 10. It's a shit time for a birthday. It's right after the holidays, when everyone is emotionally, socially, and financially tapped out. And growing up in Texas, the weather didn't help—black ice on the roads, freezing rain, the whole moody-winter-drama vibe.

Guess how many people came to my parties? Four: my mom, my brother, my sister, and me. Not only was it the party no one attended, but every year, my mom hit me with a brutal

Sophie's Choice: "Do you want a Christmas present or a birthday present?"

Um—*excuse me?*

After years of half-hearted hugs and regifted lotion sets, I had an epiphany: I don't have to settle for a sad little January birthday anymore. My favorite month is October (see where I'm going with this?). Halloween, sweater weather, apple picking, pumpkin carving—October is iconic. The air smells like cinnamon and every leaf is like something out of a Nancy Meyer's fall montage.

So I said, *Why wait?* I threw my birthday party in October, and it was fantastic! People *actually* showed up—refreshed, excited, and not dragging their post-holiday burnout into my celebration. No more trying to rally a bunch of exhausted, slightly depressed January zombies to fake party enthusiasm.

Best decision ever.

Here's what I realized: Life may not always be fair, but we can sure as hell make it fun. And that goes for every festivity you can possibly think of. If you're a Christmas lover like me, you don't *need* to wait till December to don your fave Santa PJs or put up the twinkly lights. Wanna wear your Halloween socks in February? Why wait? Want an excuse to celebrate the week, but you're in the midst of a tedious Tuesday? Pop the bottle of bubbly anyway! Feeling a lil' spicy? Don't wait for an anniversary to wear the lingerie. Pull on that slutty bodysuit now! Even if it's not a holiday. Even if you didn't get that promotion. Do whatever you want that makes you feel alive and causes your body to stir into a little tizzy. Joy does not have a schedule. *Do not wait for permission from your calendar to celebrate your life.* It's yours for the taking. You can live it any which way you choose. Blast the music, smile a little bigger, laugh a little louder, and carry yourself with a lil' extra mischief in your eyes. Love your life. You only get one of them. Don't save the good stuff for a special occasion. Because being here is the most special occasion there is.

Turn the Mirror Back on You

No matter how much money you have, no matter how smart or how beautiful you are, you can't add days to your life. But you can certainly add life to your days.

1. What are you saving for a "special occasion"? That fancy candle? The good lingerie? The expensive bottle of champagne that's been collecting dust like it's aging for the Queen's arrival? Homie! Do you secretly think you have to *earn* joy? You don't! You are *alive,* and that is reason enough to celebrate.
2. You don't have to go full-on circus act to enjoy your life as it is. It's the little things that turn ordinary days into mini celebrations. Maybe you sip your morning coffee from a cute mug that says "I LOVE CAFFEINE AND BAD DECISIONS" or blast your favorite song so loud your neighbors think you're hosting a one-person rave. When you start treating every day like a gift—even if it's just wrapped in chaos and caffeine—you make your life a way more interesting place to be. And the people lucky enough to be around you will be like, "Wow, how do they make eating cereal look this fun?" Celebrate the small stuff, and suddenly, you're not just living life—you're throwing it a party.

Women

"A strong woman looks a challenge in the eye and gives it a wink."

—GINA CAREY, MULTI-HYPHENATE BOSS OF GOSPEL MUSIC AND FILMMAKING

Listen up, sister, this chapter is dedicated to YOU (bet ya didn't see that coming)—the ladies, the femmes, and anyone else who's ever been told to "smile more." Being a woman ain't for the faint of heart. It's like trying to solve a Rubik's Cube while someone's constantly spinning the colors. Just when you think you've got it figured out, BAM—new rules, new expectations, and somehow, you're still expected to look flawless while doing it. First periods? Horror movies. Childbirth? A full-blown action thriller. And don't even get me started on the *fashion police*—don't wear white after Labor Day, but also, wear white whenever you want, but also, make sure your nipples are covered, unless it's a nip-slip dress. Make it make sense!

We're out here living in a world that's like, "Be smart, but not *too* smart. Be pretty, but not *too* pretty. Be confident, but not *too* confident—wait, why are you being so aggressive?" The rules are exhausting, contradictory, and honestly, they sound like they were written by a group of men who've never even *seen* a woman. It's exhausting!

Yet, here we are—raising kids, running boardrooms, making homes, and making moves—all while keeping our sense of humor intact.

The reason I'm even able to write this book on empowerment is because of the absolute *legends* who came before us. The women who looked the patriarchy dead in the eye and said, "Not today, Satan." They marched, they protested, they burned bras, and they paved the way so we could strut in stilettos or sneakers. So, I'd like to lift a glass to the queens who changed the game for me the most.

Mom

Hold your hats, homies, because I'm about to tell you about the strongest woman I've ever met—my mother, Moni. Picture this: It's 1979, the Iranian Revolution is tearing through her world, and there she is, standing ten feet tall and bulletproof on the front lines. Chaos is swirling, the ground feels like it's shifting under everyone's feet, but she's not backing down. She watched in horror as a firing squad opened fire on the protesters—her best friend fell right in front of her. It changed her—but it didn't break her. If anything, it made her more determined than ever to escape.

Fast-forward to the early '80s: She's moved to America, not speaking a word of English, and raised my sister, brother, and me solo. No safety net, no trust fund, just pure grit and love. If we were hungry, somehow she'd pull half a fridge out of her purse. If I needed a last-minute costume for school—just hand her a hot glue gun and some felt, and I turned into a DIY on Pinterest before Pinterest. We were happy. We didn't have much, but I never even noticed because what she gave us, money could never buy.

At the ripe old age of ten, my brand-new bike got stolen. I was fuming, ready to launch an FBI investigation. But Mom? She just smiled and said, "They must've needed it more than you. How lucky are you that you got to help someone out." Like, WHO says that?! An absolute queen, that's who.

That was my mom's superpower: flipping any bad situation on its head and teaching me to find the silver lining. If she taught me anything, it's how to survive with style, grace, and an endless supply of humor. Now, as an adult, mothering my own three children, when I catch myself doing things the way my mother did, I couldn't feel better about myself. Here's to you, Momma—the original queen and the toughest act to follow.

Maya

If you haven't noticed, I quote Maya Angelou more than anyone in this book. She is the ultimate GOAT. Her words hit me harder than my morning espresso and make me rethink my life faster than a bad Bumble date. Ever since teenage me read *I Know Why the Caged Bird Sings* in a room plastered with New Kids on the Block posters and glitter gel pens, she's been in my corner.

One line stands out above the rest: "You may not control all the events that happen to you, but you can decide not to be reduced by them."

Let's be real—life is lifey. It's messy, unpredictable, and occasionally feels like it's personally targeting you. Like when you're already late and spill coffee on your only clean shirt, and your toddler chooses that exact moment to have a meltdown over sock seams. Or when you're starting over at forty, and society's over here like, "Shouldn't you have it all figured out by now?"

Maya's words are the reason I haven't rage-quit life to go live in a yurt somewhere off the grid. She taught me that strength isn't about looking perfect or having it all together. It's showing up, scars and all, and shining anyway. Grace and grit are a package deal. That's the essence of what it means to be a woman. You embrace your truth, you roll with life's punches, and when the curveballs come flying, you learn how to swing.

Between Maya teaching me to stand tall and my mom showing me how to laugh through the mess, I've become a hopeful, over-caffeinated, chaos-embracing queen who can find the silver lining in pretty much anything.

When one sister succeeds, we all succeed. The glass ceiling has been shattered many times by one of us, and as Maya noted, "Each time a woman stands up for herself, she stands up for women everywhere." In other words, this thing called life isn't just about you. It's about us, how we show up for each other, help each other, push each other to be the best versions of ourselves as much as possible. It's about the late-night texts that say, "You got this," the shared recipes that never turn out right but we pretend taste amazing anyway, and the silent nods of solidarity when someone's being talked over in a meeting. It's about the mentors who lift us up, the friends who remind us to laugh when we'd rather cry, and the strangers who become sisters because they just *get it*.

So, here's to you: the multitaskers juggling a thousand things at once (and somehow not dropping the baby, the laptop, or the coffee). The dreamers who dare to imagine a world where equality isn't a fight but a given. The career crushers breaking barriers and building bridges for the next generation. The homebodies creating safe spaces where love and laughter thrive. The adventurers chasing horizons and proving that fear is just a suggestion. The advocates who use their voices to amplify the silenced. And the just-trying-to-figure-it-outers who remind us that it's OK not to have all the answers—because sometimes, the journey *is* the answer. You are all making this world a better, brighter, more badass place, one day at a time. Here's to us—the messy, magical, unstoppable force that we are. Cheers, queens.

Turn the Mirror Back on You

We might not get to hang out and overshare like it's a 2003 sleepover, but there's something powerful about being around your best girl. It's like charging your soul's battery. Here's how to tap into that deep, ride-or-die connection.

1. Do you celebrate your friends' successes as if they were your own, or do you let comparison sneak in? Listen, Jealous Jan, there's a difference between being inspired and turning into a green-eyed monster when your bestie gets that promotion. Her win is a win for the team. Oprah doesn't get salty when Beyoncé wins an award, and neither should you.
2. Do you make an effort to reach out and connect, even when life gets busy, or do you let your friendships fall

by the wayside? Don't be the friend who only pops up when Mercury is in retrograde. A quick check-in, or even a "Hey, I saw this meme and thought of you," can make all the difference.

3. Are you showing up for your friends consistently, even when it's inconvenient, or only when it's easy? Anyone can be there when brunch plans involve bottomless mimosas, but true friendship is about showing up when your friend needs emergency ice cream because she's been ghosted.
4. Stop the "mean girl" energy. If you catch yourself tearing down other women, cut that out. Society wired us to side-eye anyone who colors outside the lines—but you're better than that. Be the first to say hi to the new mom at school drop-off. Pass out compliments like Costco samples. And for the love of oat milk lattes, ditch the gossip. Get curious, be kind, and connect—building each other up is way more fun than tearing anyone down.

Xs

"Men are all alike—except the one you've met who's different."

—MAE WEST, THE OG QUEEN OF SASS

Ahhhh, men! Can't live with 'em, and can't live with 'em. We have fifty-one chapters dedicated to how amazing we are, so let's have one chapter dedicated to the opposing gender. From the slightly round-faced boyfriend in elementary school to some of the more musky-smelling, square-jawed paramours of the past, relationships with men, romantic or not, have served a purpose.

Shit Relationships Still Bring Valuable Glow-Ups

Every relationship is like a song you've tucked away in your memory. Sometimes you hear a particular tune, and it makes you smile, and other times, you change it to something else and think, *How the fuck was I into this shit?* You can honor how much you've grown by visiting your "playlist" from time to time.

> To Mr. Situationship—
>
> Were you real? You felt real—close enough to be something, distant enough to be nothing. We could banter for hours, flirt like we were starring in a rom-com, and still somehow I was single. Iconic.
>
> You were the leading man in a story I wrote alone, while you played the role of "emotionally unavailable" to perfection. Bravo.
>
> Therapists love you—you're a textbook case with footnotes on "avoidant attachment" and "intimacy issues." Turns out, your inability to commit was never my burden to carry, though I hauled it like unpaid overtime. And when you faded into the background like credits rolling after a forgettable film, something clicked: I'd been casting the wrong star.
>
> So, I became my own leading lady. My own date, my own soulmate, my own everything. You were unreliable, unavailable, and unforgettable. You were a masterclass in self-love, and for that, I can only say…thank you.

To Mr. Wino—

You came into my life with charm that burned warm and fast, like a cheap candle in a power outage—unreliable, but just bright enough to keep me hopeful. You were smooth, rich, and intoxicating in the beginning, like the first sip of something strong after a long day. But you aged poorly.

You taught me the art of timing—not in the romantic way, but in the when-to-say-what-so-things-don't-explode way. I learned that honesty doesn't have to be a wrecking ball if you use it with care. But you never bothered with that—you preferred to hurl your words like punches after your third glass of whatever was closest.

You made me resourceful. I learned how to fix things—broken appliances, flat tires, and eventually, myself. You were too in love with your liquid muse to notice, but I was busy becoming someone who could stand steady on her own, no bottle required.

Most of all, you taught me acceptance—the hard, unsentimental kind. You were only ever capable of meeting me where you were, which was somewhere deep in the bottom of a glass. I had to stop waiting for you to surface.

So, Mr. Wino, I raise a glass—not to you, but to the woman I became because of you. You were the mess, and I was the cleanup crew. And damn, I did a good job.

Dear Every Man Who Has Taught Me Something

You arrived in all shapes—fathers, brothers, friends, exes, Uber drivers who became therapists on late-night rides home. Some of you stayed, some disappeared, and some left marks that took years to fade. You were gentle or cruel, wise or clueless, fleeting or forever. You taught me in whispers, in shouts, in silences that roared.

You taught me to set boundaries—not the polite kind, but the kind built from tears and sleepless nights. You made me speak up when I wanted to stay quiet and take leaps when standing still felt safer. You held up a mirror, and even when I hated what I saw, you forced me to look.

Loving you—platonically, passionately, disastrously—left me wiser, tougher, softer. You stretched my heart until it ached, then taught me how to hold it steady on my own. To believe in love, but only if I'm in the front row, not sitting on the sidelines hoping to be seen.

Would I relive it all again? Hell no. I'd sooner tickle a hungry lion's balls than take another spin through certain chapters. But still—thank you. You were the reason I learned what better looks like—and why I never settle for less.

Turn the Mirror Back on You

I know it's hard to be thankful for the total dumpster fire that is our former love life, but if we can change our perspective, we can find the value in a failed relationship. And that's the gift that keeps on giving.

1. At some point, you had to make the hardest, most important decision: to love yourself more than the idea of "making it work." And you did. Be proud of that. You'll never settle for less just to keep a Tom, Dick, or Harry around. You chose *you*—and that's a love story that never ends.
2. You learned you don't need to have a partner to make you happy. *You* are responsible for your one and only happiness! Your mood is not determined by someone else's—that's a fucking lottery-ticket win, right there.
3. You've experienced the fucking oxygen thief who sucks all the air out of the room, but now you choose people who are secure enough to let you be fully you. Finding someone who loves every messy, magical part of you? That's like coming home—to yourself.

X Factor

"Find out who you are and do it on purpose."

—COUNTRY MUSIC'S FAIRY GODMOTHER IN HEELS HIGHER THAN MY STANDARDS, DOLLY PARTON

Let's talk about her—the woman with the X factor. She's not just walking into a room; she's *arriving*. Heads turn, conversations pause, and even the universe seems to straighten its tie and pay attention. The X factor isn't about having perfect hair or wearing clothes that scream "expensive." It's about something much deeper—something you can't buy, borrow, or fake. It's that electric mix of confidence, charm, and authenticity that makes people say, "I'll have what she's having."

The X Factor Isn't What You Think

Contrary to popular belief, the X factor has nothing to do with looking like a Victoria's Secret model or having a million Instagram followers who double-tap your avocado toast posts. It's about how you make people feel when you enter a space. It's presence. It's alignment. It's the woman in the corner of the coffee shop, calmly sipping her latte, radiating a quiet power without needing to speak a word. It's the way she makes eye contact—like she's seen enough to know who she is, and doesn't need to prove it.

She's not trying to stand out. She already does. She's not chasing attention—it naturally finds her. Because when a woman is deeply rooted in herself, in her truth, in her energy, she doesn't just take up space.

She elevates it.

What the X Factor Really Looks Like

The X factor woman knows who she is—and more importantly, who she isn't. She's not trying to win the approval of every stranger she meets. She's too busy living instead of chasing validation. She's the friend who hypes you up at a party like she's getting paid for it. "That dress? A moment! That walk? Deadly. Your ex? May he trip over a charger cord."

She's the coworker who handles chaos with grace—printer jam, surprise client call, and spilled coffee? No problem. She takes a deep breath, tosses her hair like she's in a shampoo commercial, and gets shit done.

Confidence Without Cockiness

A little insider tip? The X factor isn't something people are born with—it's earned. The X factor woman has been through it. She's had her heart broken by people she thought would never hurt her, lost jobs she thought she couldn't live without, and faced rejection so sharp it could carve ice sculptures. But she turned every setback into a comeback.

She's the CEO of her own life—and sometimes that life looks like closing a million-dollar deal, and other times, it's just getting through a Monday with only one emotional breakdown. She knows she's *that girl*—not because she needs attention, but because she knows her value. She doesn't compete. She claps. When she wins, she celebrates. And when her friends win? She celebrates even louder.

Self-Awareness Is Her Superpower

The woman with the X factor isn't perfect—but she's *present*.

She's cried over men who vlogged their protein shakes, survived toxic group chats, and once paid $300 for a psychic who vanished after telling her she'd meet her soulmate "any day now." And she owns every second of it. She's learning. She's unlearning. She's evolving, even on the days when she's just getting by.

She's not trying to have all the answers—she's focused on asking better questions. She knows life doesn't require her to be flawless. It just asks her to show up.

So who is this magnetic, grounded, unforgettable woman?

Who is this woman so secure in her softness and her fire?

The X factor woman…is you.

Turn the Mirror Back on You

Want to tap into your X factor? I guarantee you won't have to look too hard.

1. Start your day like you're the main character: Whether it's blasting your hype song or sipping your latte like it's a cinematic moment, walk like the world is giving you a standing ovation.
2. Make eye contact like a CEO: Whether you're at preschool drop-off or a board meeting, own the room with eye contact that says, "I've got this."
3. What are your strengths? Don't downplay them! Maybe you tell the best dirty jokes, write thank-you notes like it's your love language, or can charm a room in seconds. Hell, even ear-flapping counts! Whatever it is—it's yours. Own your magic.
4. Stuck figuring out your strengths? Think back to moments you felt truly proud—even if it's from when you were five and rescued a roly-poly. Congrats, you're officially a life-saving ninja. Now ask why those moments mattered. Did they show your compassion, resilience, or that killer sense of humor that lifts the room when things get heavy? Whatever they are, treasure them. They're what make you, you.

Yes! to Life After Having Kids

"Nothing has a stronger influence psychologically on their environment and especially on their children than the unlived life of the parent."

—CARL JUNG, ONCE FREUD'S STAR STUDENT, UNTIL THEY GOT INTO A PSYCHOLOGICAL HISSY FIT—THEN HE BROKE OFF AND HELPED FOUND MODERN THERAPY, BLENDING DREAMS, ARCHETYPES, AND A WHOLE LOT OF SOUL-SEARCHING.

Now, darlings, gather round. I'm going to spin you a tale about the one and only—you. Little did you know, you stepped out into the world like a female Samuel L. Jackson, oozing confidence and effortlessly strutting your stuff with your perky, un-breastfed tits held high in the air.

Then, one chilly October morn, as you lay in bed, hungover from a fabulous tequila-soaked night with the girls, aliens abducted you. They took you back to their invisible ship, gathered around you, and chanted, "You are the chosen one." Then, they gave you a lobotomy and dropped you back into your bed, leaving no evidence in sight.

The next morning, you woke up at thirty-five, married with three children, a minivan, and a Costco membership—and life as you knew it was over. Your thoughts no longer revolved around yourself. The only things occupying your mind now were: *Did the baby poop?* and *Laundry is my favorite.*

Let's pause for a moment of silence for all the fun-filled nights we lost…due to the aliens…

Break the Martyr Mom Cycle

You've spent the last decade hitting the "pause" button on you. "No, I can't go out—Sam has a fever, and Sasha needs her hair braided." Sound familiar? When's the last time you said yes to yourself?

Back when you were younger, you didn't overthink—you dreamed. You took chances. You didn't worry about car payments, bills, or perfectly timed school drop-offs. You lived boldly, tits held high in the air, ready for adventure.

But as you became an adult, you started collecting responsibilities like they were high-valued stamps—mortgages, deadlines, soccer practice schedules, and the eternal quest for the perfect slow cooker recipe. You turned into a "grown-up," trading spontaneity for spreadsheets and wild nights for early bedtimes. You chose a life that ranges from "meh" to "aggressively average," all because you put everyone else first. And you're not alone, because I fell prey to it, too.

It's time to remember who you were before life got so damn busy. You think you're doing your kids a favor by putting yourself last, but even Carl Jung believed that unfulfilled dreams don't just disappear—they boomerang back into your children's lives wearing a name tag that says, " Hi, I'm unresolved baggage and need therapy." Ask yourself: "Would I want my child to live the life I'm living now?" If the answer's "yes," write a memoir. If not, keep reading.

If you're living like a stressed-out martyr, guess what they're learning? That self-sacrifice is the ultimate goal. That dreams are for other people. That life is about surviving, not thriving. But if they see you chasing dreams, picking up hobbies, or launching your Etsy empire during nap time, they learn something far more powerful: that life doesn't end when the baby monitor turns on.

When you pursue your passions, your kids get front-row seats to adventures they wouldn't otherwise experience. Maybe your passion is travel—suddenly, family vacations become epic cultural quests, not just trips to the same beach every summer. Or perhaps you're into art, and your dining table turns into a mini Picasso studio. A mom who's passionate about cooking might turn Taco Tuesday into a global culinary tour. A mom who hikes introduces her kids to nature, teaching them that Mother Nature puts on a better show than any iPad ever could.

Maybe you watched your own mom put herself last, thinking that's what "good moms" do. It's not. Your kids will copy what they see, so show them that pursuing joy and ambition isn't just OK—*it's essential.*

Motherhood isn't about vanishing into your kids' schedules—it's about bringing your whole, vibrant self into the mix. I don't mean having a coke bender in the school bathroom during your youngster's Christmas concert, but being an adult doesn't mean losing out on the fun. And how are you going to teach your children to follow their dreams and set their true north to "yes" if you don't follow yours? When you live fully, you teach your kids to do the same. A mom who loves her life shows her kids how to love theirs. That's the real legacy—not just love, but a life well lived.

You Get Playdates, Too

When I started unchaining myself from my children, it came with a bit of an adjustment for us all. My boys couldn't have cared less. So long as there was food, they were happy. But the warden, a.k.a. my daughter, felt differently. One night in a land far, far away (my living room), Violet decided to lay it on thick: "Whaddya doing? I didn't say you could go out. Don't you love me anymore? Go back to the kitchen and make me a plate of Goldfish and Little Bites.?"

To which I instantly replied, "Listen, Undertaker of the Forgotten, don't *you* have playdates? Does that mean you don't love me?" Now, when I decide to unchain myself from Goldfish and Little Bites, Violet knows it's just Mommy saying yes to herself.

You only get one life. Remember who you were before the abduction. Say yes to life and walk around with your tits held high…again.

Turn the Mirror Back on You

Let's go back and find the dreamer in you. Here are some things to help you get reacquainted with the "you" before the diapers and nap schedules.

1. Turn errands into mini escapes. Need to pick up groceries? Pop in your favorite podcast, grab an iced latte, and make it *your* time. Who knew errands could feel like self-care?
2. Model the life you want for your kids: Be the role model you wish you had. Pursue that side hustle; take that class. Take the opportunity at every moment to reach for a life that's more "yes" and less "meh." Show your kids that life doesn't stop when they arrive—it expands.
3. When you go out, do not put the phone on the table! I'm not saying don't check in with the lil' squirts, but allow yourself to get lost in a good time.

Yin/Yang

"You can be tough and tender. Fierce and kind. You don't have to pick one—you're allowed to be both."

—BRENÉ BROWN. HER NETFLIX SPECIALS HIT LIKE A CHRIS ROCK SET—BUT INSTEAD OF JOKES, SHE READS YOUR SOUL LIKE IT OWES HER MONEY.

Life isn't about being one thing—it's about being everything. You're bold and soft, driven and playful, logical yet wildly creative. You're the fierce parallel-parking warrior *and* the sap who cries at puppy commercials. That's called range. This balance—the yin and the yang, the masculine and the feminine—is where your magic lives.

The Masculine and Feminine Energy Breakdown

Masculine and feminine energies aren't about gender; they're about traits and vibes. Think of your *masculine energy* as your inner CEO—she's the boss who makes lists, crushes goals, and carries all the groceries in one trip like a human forklift. She's not afraid to order takeout without reading the menu and asks for the manager in a "we're going to solve this problem my way" kind of way.

Your *feminine energy* is your artsy bestie who feels all the feelings, lights candles "for the vibe," and makes impulse buys from Instagram ads. She knows when to pause and sip her chai latte "just because," and daydreams about running away to Italy but settles for an extra-long shower instead. You *need* both of them.

When Masculine and Feminine Energy Team Up

Separately, your energies can be like an episode of *The Real Housewives of Atlanta*—chaotic and impossible to manage. But together, they become a power duo—like peanut butter and jelly or moms and dry shampoo. They balance each other out, smoothing over life's rough patches like emotional spackle.

When these energies team up, you can juggle deadlines, remember birthdays, and still make a last-minute volcano for the science fair. You're not just surviving—you're thriving. Need to prep for a last-minute meeting while comforting a teary kid? That's yin and yang. Hosting a family gathering while texting your work team about deadlines? Balance in action. You're the human version of a Swiss Army Knife—adaptable, efficient, and weirdly good at popping corks.

From Burnout to Balance

When a woman leans too hard into her masculine energy, she's basically a one-woman SWAT team. She's scheduling back-to-back meetings like she's running a Fortune 500 company and firing off emails with "per my last email" energy—highly efficient but zero chill. She's so deep in boss mode she might forget she has feelings until Adele's "Easy on Me" comes on—and suddenly she's sobbing over a broken dishwasher like it personally betrayed her. She's a power suit with a side of burnout.

On the flip side, if she's swimming too far into her feminine, she's basically starring in her own rom-com—dreamily lighting candles, journaling about her intentions, and "manifesting" a pay raise without actually asking for one. She's got more crystals than sense and deadlines. She's soft and flowy—until the Wi-Fi goes out, and suddenly her inner drill sergeant snaps back to life.

Life isn't about picking sides—it's about blending them. Tap into your masculine energy when you need to get stuff done, and lean into your feminine energy when you need to feel and connect. You're allowed to be both, all the time, unapologetically.

So go ahead—write that business plan and journal about your feelings. The yin and yang inside you aren't in competition—they're your ultimate power couple.

Turn the Mirror Back on You

Here's the fun part—you already have both energies inside you. Here's how to tap into both without losing your mind.

1. Bust out that planner and use your masculine energy to structure your week like a productivity queen. Then, use your feminine energy to know when to ditch the plan and binge-watch a true-crime doc when your soul needs a break.
2. Practice sending that "per my last email" message without the passive-aggressive tone. Every word is a

reflection of yourself. Say what you mean—but sprinkle a little grace on top.

3. Goals are amazing. Paint that masterpiece or write that book—but set a deadline and hold yourself accountable. Vision boards are cute, but execution is what gets you there.

Zero Fucks

"Maturity is what happens when one learns to only give a fuck about what's truly fuckworthy."

—MARK MANSON, THE FOUL MOUTHED PHILOSOPHER WE DIDN'T KNOW WE NEEDED

Congratulations, fuckface! Not only have you almost made it to the end of this book, but you're at that #FuckIt phase of your life during which zero fucks are given! Some days you're Mother Teresa, and other days you're a motherfucker—but the bottom line is, you now own all parts of yourself without apology!

Up until this point, your friends and family have had a million ideas about what's right for you. And you know what they say about opinions? Yup, cornholes. They're stinky, unwanted, and unless they match yours, get 'em away! Up until now, you've been giving out fucks like popcorn at the movies. But not anymore. The tides have changed, and you're no longer giving out your fucks for free. You're saving them for things that are worthy.

"How the fuck am I supposed to know what's worthy?" you might be asking. Well, like anything else, it's trial and error. It's falling off the horse and getting back on the saddle. *Life is lifey.* And face it: *We're* messy. Could we ask for anything less of ourselves? Our beauty is complex, heartbreaking, incomparable—it's the creative force of the universe.

You Got One Life

It was 2018. Jay Rock's "Win" was blasting at Bootsy Bellows on Sunset Boulevard—full chaos energy, little lime, *a lot* of tequila. Somewhere between the DJ dropping bangers and the bartender ignoring my very clear eye contact, Kevin Hart leaned in and yelled in my ear:

"You got one life! You gotta live your life!"

Now before your mind goes there—*no*, this wasn't a smash fest. His wife was right next to him, and Kevin and I had been friends since 2000. We'd worked together, laughed together, and—on my end—bitched about the same life crisis for years.

That night, I was once again spiraling. Telling him how stuck I felt, how I was living under my potential, how my dreams were slipping away like a drunk girl's Uber at 2:00 a.m.

He just looked at me, laughed, and said, "Shahi! You've been saying the same shit for as long as I've known you! Stop worrying about what other people think. Do *you*. You gotta live your life. You got one life!"

You are this awesome. *You* are the main character in your story. Not your husband, not your children, not your mother. You. You. YOU. You are the cat's meow, and you have *one* life, so you gotta live it. You're not going to get a second chance at any of this shit. Your passion and belief in the kind of life you want should be bigger than your fear. But no one is going to hand it to you, sister. You need to have the guts to live each moment as truthfully as you can, and the things you want will start to appear. #ZeroFucks

My hope for you is that, as you read this, you feel the sense of confidence that comes from being comfortable in your skin and knowing exactly who you are. You've probably lived through a few different phases in your life, but your identity is solid. Hell, maybe some part of you is still searching, but at this point, it's not for something you think is missing inside of you—it's for the fun and fulfillment you know you deserve. No fucks wasted on anything else.

As soon as I stopped living in accordance with what others wanted me to do, I was floating through life, like my feet barely touched the ground. Yes, I lost some friends along the way. But guess what? *I didn't give a fuck*. I was finally doing me. Adios, fuckwads. I still don't miss you. It's time to do life on my own terms!

And it's time to celebrate, because now, you're doing it, too. You know what works for you and what doesn't. You're OK if people don't like you. You're fine with being different. You're blazing your own trail, despite passive-aggressive questions from Aunt Betty that cut like knives while she's pretending to care. Naturally, some fucks are worth giving, but now, *you* decide where to spend your fucking currency. The dick in the Prius who cut you off, or your ex-husband's girlfriend's profile picture, or Aunt Betty saying, "What? You didn't know that the whole neighborhood is talking about you?" do not make the cut.

I know it's scary, but you're now as brave as the first man who tried an oyster. Perfection is not the goal. Doing what other people think you should do is not the goal. Being authentic is what's cool now. Reinvention, especially if you're doing it with children, ain't for sissies—but when you give zero fucks, you have way more energy than you thought possible. Energy you can put toward building the life you were always meant to live.

Not one person on this vast and expansive planet has walked in your shoes before. Do you, whatever that looks like. You know you're a bad bitch, and the people who really count love you for it. Don't look back. You're not going that way.

Turn the Mirror Back on You

Getting to the point where you have no more fucks to give takes practice. The tips below will help you along that road to a stress-free, worry-free way of being.

1. Be picky with your fucks. You only have so much emotional energy—don't waste it on every random opinion that flies your way. Care about what actually matters—your values, your goals, and the people who love you even when you ugly-cry.
2. Stop trying to make everyone like you. Trying to be liked by everyone is like chasing Wi-Fi at a music festival—impossible. Being yourself means some people will not vibe with you—and that's a them problem, not a you problem.
3. Don't let rejection, in any area, discourage you. Rejection = proof you're trying. It isn't a red flag—it's a badge of honor. It means you're putting yourself out there,

which is more than most people can say. Every "no" is just making space for a better "yes."

4. Define success your way! Stop living for clout or likes. What makes you feel accomplished? Maybe it's crushing a work deadline—or just surviving another PTA meeting. Success isn't a Pinterest board; it's whatever makes your heart actually happy.

Zoom Out

"When you change the way you look at things, the things you look at change."

—WAYNE DYER, THE SPIRITUAL BIG BROTHER WE ALL WISH WE HAD—PART SAGE, PART DAD-JOKE ENTHUSIAST, ROCKING A HAWAIIAN SHIRT AND SIPPING TEA

Let's face it: Life rips sometimes. You picked up this book because you've been riding the struggle bus for too long, and it's time to switch to the awesome train. I know the transition is hard and messy, but life is a full-contact sport, and you've gotta suit up if you want to play.

But amongst the hard and the messy, it's important to zoom out and find perspective. And no, I'm not talking about the kind of philosophical musing that questions why people put pets in strollers or pineapple on pizza (no to both). I mean the kind of grounded perspective that kicks in when life is pelting you with lemons and you're out here trying to make lemonade.

Whenever I feel like I'm kissing rock bottom, I try to zoom out and take a bird's eye view. I look at my life as if it's a play (I'm an actor, just go with me), and all the plot twists, the heroes, the villains, the ghosters, the glam squads, and the gut punches are just teachers I've cast to help me grow into the best version of myself.

So I ask: "What is this moment teaching me?" Is it to speak up? To be more selective with who gets access to me? To stop saying yes when I mean no?

Looking at it this way reminds me that I'm not a victim of my circumstances—I'm a creator. And if I had the power to create this mess, then I have the power to change it. Existential crisis averted!

Zooming out helps you hear that inner voice—the one that swoops in and whispers, "Girl, it's not like you lost a kidney. Breathe. You've got this." Because most things, even the seemingly catastrophic ones, are either temporary or changeable.

Sister, you have to ask yourself: "Will this matter in a week? A month? A year?" If the answer is "no," you're probably safe to unclench your jaw, exhale, and keep it moving. And if the answer is "yes," then reach down into your soul and fight to make the changes necessary. You will always have your back.

The hits aren't here to take you out—they're here to teach you how to win. So, no need for a pity party (they're boring, and no one ever brings cake). It's bright side or bust. As Alphonse Karr said, "We can complain because rose bushes have thorns, or rejoice because thorns have roses." Both are true. But you get to choose which story you tell yourself.

Now let's be honest, there will always be worries lurking in the corners of your brain like, "Will I grow chin hair?" or "Did these pockets just make my vagina look fat?" But when you zoom out, you can laugh at those thoughts for what they are—minor blips in the grand scheme of your gloriously chaotic, completely unique life.

And while you're at it, don't forget to soak up the good stuff! The little joys that sneak up on you when you're not even paying attention.

That first sip of coffee in the morning when your brain finally boots up. The smell after it rains—clean, fresh, like the universe just hit "refresh." The unexpected joy of finding five bucks in your coat pocket. Your kids laughing *together* instead of fighting over who hit who first. These moments are everywhere. Tiny bursts of magic. Little signs that life is still good, even when it's messy.

You are the writer, the director, and the star of your story. No one else gets to hold the pen unless you hand it to them. And once you realize how much power you hold, you'll never feel helpless again.

Turn the Mirror Back on You

1. We love to turn our lives into a telenovela. Before turning on the waterworks, really look at your situation and see what it's teaching you. The universe constantly conspires in our favor, pushing us towards growth when we least expect it. Find the lesson.
2. Gratitude is the attitude for everything in life. Even if the house is burning down, be grateful you made it out alive. I once read that if we all put our problems out on

the table, we'd take ours back in a heartbeat. There are many who would give anything to be going through the struggles you currently are.

3. Maybe you need a change of environment in order to see things clearly. New surroundings bring new perspectives. Sometimes we stay in the same space mentally because we are living the same patterns over and over again. Whether you need to take a walk, a long drive, or even just move to a different room, it can provide you with the clarity to see things differently. Your journey is full of highs, lows, and in between. There will be moments of unexpected joy that make everything worth it. And, when all else fails, there's always pizza. Life! Amirite?!

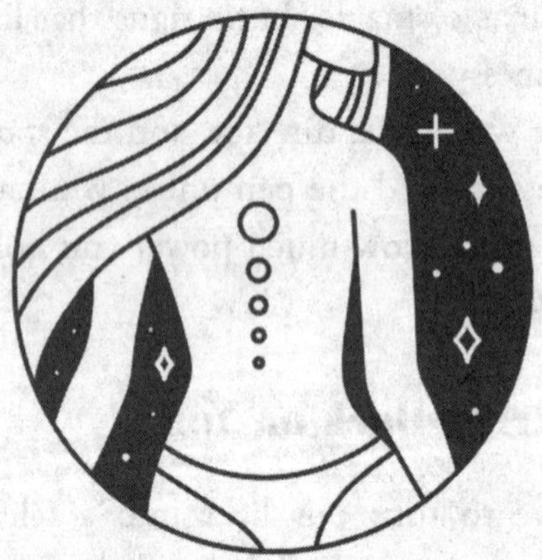

Sister, life is constantly calling us to step up and shape the future we want. And sometimes the only way to do that is to zoom out and ask yourself, "Does the story I'm telling support the life I want to create?"

You have one life. It's never too late. Day one could be today. *All you have to do is decide.*